A GUIDE TO WRITING SOCIOLOGY PAPERS

Second Edition

The Sociology Writing Group
University of California, Los Angeles

Coordinators and Editors:
Judith Richlin-Klonsky and Ellen Strenski

Authors: ROSEANN GIARRUSSO

                 JUDITH RICHLIN-KLONSKY

                 WILLIAM G. ROY

                 ELLEN STRENSKI

Contributors: CONSTANCE COINER

                 ARLENE DALLALFAR

                 LISA FROHMANN

                 NANCY A. MATTHEWS

ILLUSTRATIONS BY HANNAH BALTER

ST. MARTIN'S PRESS   NEW YORK

Project management: Omega Publishing Services, Inc.
Cover design: Jehaber & Peace, Inc.
Cover photo: David M. Grossman

Library of Congress Catalog Card Number: 89-63935
Manufactured in the United States of America.
54321
fedcba

For information, write St. Martin's Press, Inc.
175 Fifth Ave., New York, N.Y. 10010

ISBN: 0-312-03651-5

TO THE INSTRUCTOR

The quality of student writing is a constant concern to college teachers. Like their colleagues in other disciplines, many sociology instructors, preoccupied by the demands of their profession and dreading the likelihood of poorly written or perhaps plagiarized papers, despair of assigning writing and rely instead on tests. But to do so deprives students of the active, personal engagement with sociological concepts and data that only writing about them can provide. This book is an attempt to do something about this problem.

A Guide to Writing Sociology Papers grew out of our collective experiences as sociology and English faculty members, teaching assistants, counselors, and tutors at UCLA. The book is designed to relieve you of some of the burden of writing instruction and to provide your students—from beginning to advanced—with practical advice. Its format is flexible enough to accommodate specific modifications, yet "spelled out" enough to guide those who need to pay special attention to all steps in the writing process, from initial conceptualization to final presentation.

The underlying premise of the book is that thinking and writing are integrally related—that is, to write a sociology paper is to exercise the "sociological imagination." Our advice and examples are informed throughout by this practical pedagogical observation. For example, when instructors comment to students that their papers "are too psychological" or "really didn't address a sociological issue," students tend to be confused and rarely know how to correct the problem in later papers. Similarly, comments that a paper "has no structure," "follows no clear logic," or "lacks sufficient evidence" often baffle students. Our goal here is to provide both you and your students with illustrations and a common language for discussing and improving papers in these areas.

The book can be used in a variety of ways in both lower- and upper-division sociology courses. It can simply be assigned as a reference for students to consult on their own. You can refer in class or in discussion sections to specific parts when you mention papers, explaining how students can apply our advice to your assignment and how our sample student papers do or do not represent what you expect. Or, in comments on drafts or in individual conferences with students, you can refer students to specific pages in the text.

This book can also be used in a range of writing classes from remedial to advanced. It is especially appropriate for adjunct writing courses paired with sociology courses. However, since much of the advice we present can be generalized to other disciplines, it is also suitable as a basic text in advanced writing courses emphasizing the social sciences. Much of the book—Chapters 2, 3, 5, 6, 7, and Part III—applies equally to the humanities.

While we focus on priorities most commonly identified by instructors, our own writing style is intentionally "student-friendly." Students report that learning about writing is sometimes boring, and for some intimidating. Thus, our tone is deliberately easygoing, avoiding prohibitions where possible, including contractions where they soften the prose, and offering guidelines rather than commandments. We also include many specific examples, some taken from student papers, to make the guidelines less abstract.

Acknowledgments

A climate favorable to a project such as ours has been created at the University of California, Los Angeles, by UCLA Writing Programs, the Academic Advancement Program, the Academic Resource Center, and the UCLA reference librarians. We appreciate their continuing support of our common efforts.

Production of the pamphlet on which this book is based was funded by the UCLA Office of Instructional Development. The UCLA Department of Sociology and UCLA Writing Programs provided supplementary clerical support.

We thank Jeffrey Alexander and Melvin Pollner, both of UCLA, for their help in locating appropriate student papers. Special thanks go to the student authors themselves—Lysa Agundez, Ellen Berlfein, Sandra Ducoff Garber, and Alvin Hasegawa—for their permission to use their work as examples.

Alice M. Roy, Coordinator of the Writing Program at California State University, Los Angeles, made helpful suggestions on "Logic and Structure" in the first chapter. Several members of the Department of Sociology, UCLA, provided valuable comments on earlier drafts of Part II: Robert M. Emerson and Linda L. Shaw ("Ethnographic Field

Research"); Kenneth Bailey and Gina Randolph ("Quantitative Research"). Professor Emerson also generously granted permission to adapt sections of the guidelines on ethnographic field research he distributes to his students.

Michael Weber, sociology editor in the College Division of St. Martin's Press, recognized the widespread need for a book such as this, and our group is grateful for his support. Charles Briel, St. Martin's sales representative in our area, also deserves our thanks, as does Anne McCoy, project editor for the book. Saul Feinman, of the University of Wyoming, provided an unusually thorough review of the manuscript in which he offered excellent suggestions about the shape it should take.

Above all, this book could not have been conceived or created without the innumerable sociology students whose writing processes we have shared as instructors, tutors, teaching assistants, counselors, and writing consultants. We have been enriched by their efforts to expand their sociological imaginations and to convey their new insights and knowledge in written form.

A Note about the Second Edition

This edition updates the sample student papers. We have added information about computers, not just about word processing, but about the computer's outlining capabilities, and the pros and cons of a computerized literature search. Sample ethnographic field notes are included in this edition, as is a sample instrument for the sample quantitative paper. We have revised the chapter on writing to reflect more comprehensively the entire writing process, including outlining and stylistic revision. Particularly important is the new information on critical thinking and reading, and its connection with writing. That emphasis is reflected in Part II's revised chapter order, which now begins with textual analysis.

We appreciate the guidance and encouragement of Debra Nesbitt, who saw the book through its transition to a second edition during her tenure as sociology editor at St. Martin's Press.

The Sociology Writing Group

CONTENTS

TO THE STUDENT

If you're uneasy about the prospect of writing a sociology paper, you're not alone. Many students feel as you do; that's why we wrote this book. We can't promise that your assignment will be easy, but it *can* be done, and done well. This book can help you feel in control of the writing process from beginning to end, and it can help you produce your best work.

We've written the guide we wish we'd had as undergraduates. We learned too late what "explicate" means. We didn't know how to include our field notes. We had to return to the library at the last minute to find page numbers for passages we needed to cite because we neglected to jot them down in the first place, and we experienced many other problems in writing our own papers. We want to spare you some of the trouble we endured. And we have learned that procrastination—our own and that of others—is not always the result of laziness but often a sign of uncertainty about just how to begin and complete a given writing task.

Our students often tell us that they don't know what they're expected to do in a paper or that they don't know what the instructor wants. So we've tried to demystify the whole process. For example, we explain in Chapter 1 what makes a sociology paper different from papers in other disciplines and what sociology instructors want in terms of a paper's logic and structure. We suggest ways to get started and to stay on track, ways to deal with and present your data, and ways to troubleshoot your writing and to make your prose professional. All along the way our book gives practical illustrations, including some sample student papers you can match with your own. These papers are very good but not perfect. We have commented on their fine features and suggested alternatives where they illustrate problems.

We recommend that everyone read Part I on "Essentials" and Part III on "Finishing Up." Chapters in Part II, "Writing from Various

1

Data Sources," can be used selectively. Use the table of contents and the index to look up what you need.

In Part I, Chapter 1 begins with the conceptual starting points which are fundamental for writing a good sociology paper. Chapters 2, 3, 4, and 5, respectively, present basic guidelines about organizing your time; writing and revising, keeping track of citations, notes, and references; and avoiding plagiarism. Follow these guidelines from the beginning of your project.

Treat Part II on "Writing from Various Data Sources" as a reference tool. Read the introduction, and then delve into the individual chapters as you need them. These chapters cover four typical kinds of sociology papers that are, in turn, based on four different data sources: the textual analysis paper (Chapter 6), the library research paper (Chapter 7), the ethnographic field research paper (Chapter 8), and the quantitative research paper (Chapter 9). The chapter on library research includes a list of specialized sociological reference sources, and the other three chapters contain three student papers as illustrations.

Part III on "Finishing Up" is again for everyone. It contains two short but crucial chapters: a checklist to help you polish your final draft (Chapter 10) and guidelines for the last step—typing, formatting, and submitting your paper (Chapter 11).

Don't sit down and try to read the whole book at one go. Chapter 2 and all the chapters in Part II are meant to guide you through steps in a process. Use these chapters as you would instructions for assembling anything—first scan the chapter to get a sense of what you're in for and then consult it carefully as you move along step by step. Sometimes writing assignments can loom as enormous, mysterious tasks because students don't know how to break them into smaller, more manageable tasks. This guide does that for you. There may be portions of the guide that you'll have to reread before they make sense to you, and other portions that you'll refer to again and again for present and future writing assignments.

The primary purpose of this book is, of course, to help you prepare good sociology papers, and, except for Chapter 9 on quantitative research, which is more technical than the other chapters, you'll be able to use this book from day one of any sociology course. But you'll also find that much of this book applies as well to other social sciences. And many parts will even help you write papers in the humanities. So *A Guide to Writing Sociology Papers* will help you from start to finish of your college career.

Your own campus may offer other resources to help you further.

• Find out if your campus library offers tours so that you can get an overview of its organization. A short time invested at the beginning of the quarter or semester when schedules tend to be less demanding may save you many hours of wandering and wondering later.

- Find out if your English department offers composition courses in which you can practice these writing skills. Investigate writing courses even after you have fulfilled the common requirement for freshman composition. (Don't let English majors corner the market on intermediate or advanced courses.) At some colleges special writing courses are attached to sociology and other courses, a combination which benefits you doubly. If you are concerned that with your present writing skills you might not get a high grade in a composition class, check out the possibility of taking it as an elective on a pass/no pass basis.
- Find out if your campus has a tutoring center where peer or professional tutors can review your work with you and help you strengthen your skills.

A Note on Our Writing Style

Before going on, we would like you to note two features of our writing: our occasional use of contractions (for example, "we've" instead of "we have") and our avoidance of sexist language.

First, we have tried to make this book as down-to-earth and practical as possible. We imagine ourselves talking to you as we talk to our own students—trying to be direct, friendly, and helpful. Our prose is therefore rather informal and includes contractions. Academic papers, on the other hand, have a different purpose and are usually more formal. Some instructors might object to your using contractions in a sociology paper.

Second, we have deliberately used inclusive language when we refer to people in general. Historically, masculine nouns and pronouns have been used to refer to women and men both—for example, "*Man* is a social animal." As a result of the women's movement, this usage is slowly changing. The checklist in Chapter 10 explains ways of avoiding sexist language.

Finally, we wish we could show you some of our drafts of this book. Writing anything worthwhile—a paper or a book—is always a messy, frustrating, creative, and finally rewarding process. Our own experience has been typical. Final written work usually looks so neat that it's easy to forget the wastepaper baskets overflowing with outlines scribbled on scratch paper, penciled drafts, cut and pasted revisions, and annotated computer printouts. For example, the word processing program on one of our computers automatically counts the number of times a finger touches a key as each document is typed. Writing Chapter 7 involved over 80,000 keystrokes, as we typed in material, re-arranged it, changed it, added to it, replaced it, or erased it. So don't be discouraged if you don't like what you first write. That's normal. The paper will improve, and you will like it better with each succeeding keystroke or pencil mark. *A Guide to Writing Sociology Papers* will show you how this happens and will guide you through the process.

PART I

ESSENTIALS

Perhaps the most disabling myth about intellectual activity is that writing is an art that is prompted by inspiration. Some writing can be classified as an art, no doubt, but the art of writing is a trade in the same sense that plumbing or automotive repair are trades. Just as plumbers and mechanics would rarely accomplish anything if they waited for inspiration to impel them to action, so writers would rarely write if they relied on inspiration.

RODNEY STARK,
—*Sociology*

Writing is a craft as well as an art. As with any other craft, becoming a good writer requires understanding the principles of how papers work. A first-rate plumber must know some principles of hydraulics, and an outstanding auto mechanic, the principles of combustion. Writing a good sociological paper requires understanding principles of both sociology and writing.

Part I presents these fundamentals of craftsmanship. Chapter 1, "Getting Started," explains some topics that might be considered as much inspiration as perspiration, such as how to use a "sociological imagination" in writing. More specifically, this chapter covers some of the qualities that instructors look for in papers but that students sometimes have difficulty grasping. An instructor will frequently criticize student papers as being "not sufficiently sociological," "not addressing a real question," or "having problems of logic and structure." But often students are not sure what the instructor means, and instructors often find themselves at a loss how exactly to interpret their own comments. So we have explained what sociologists mean when they require papers to "take a sociological perspective," to be "logical and well structured," and to "answer a well-formed question."

Starting a paper at all and then staying on a productive schedule is troublesome for many students, so Chapter 2, "Organizing Your Time: The Time Grid," has some practical advice about this problem. Chapter 3, "The Writing Process," recommends techniques for harnessing the power of the writing process itself to trigger insights and to continually clarify your ideas. Chapter 4, "Citations, Notes, and References," shows how to acknowledge sources of information in your paper, and Chapter 5, "Avoiding Plagiarism," explains how to respect the integrity of those sources when you quote or paraphrase.

Chapter 1

GETTING STARTED

Additionally, and especially in the social sciences, much unclear writing is based on unclear or incomplete thought. It is possible with safety to be technically obscure about something you haven't thought out. It is impossible to be wholly clear on something you do not understand.

JOHN KENNETH GALBRAITH,
—*"Writing, Typing, and Economics"*

Writing a good sociology paper starts with asking a good sociological question. Picking a topic is just the beginning of planning your paper. You need to frame your paper's topic in the form of a *question*. Asking a good question will make the other tasks of writing your paper much easier and will help you hand in a good finished product.

Everything else follows from the question your paper asks. Think of taking a photograph. The deepest artistic sensitivity or the most sophisticated technical skills cannot create a beautiful picture unless you point the camera in the right direction. But carefully aiming the camera in the right direction can combine with simple competence and a personal point of view to produce a fine and, if you are lucky, breathtaking photograph. Likewise, when you create a sociology paper, you can produce interesting, high-quality results without being the smartest or most eloquent student in the world: the key is to take the time to "point" your work in an effective direction by asking a well-formulated question.

Sometimes instructors assign papers by requiring students to respond to a particular question. When that happens make sure you thoroughly understand the question and keep it in mind as you work on the paper. Not answering the instructor's question is one of the most frequent pitfalls of student writing. Even if you have a thoroughly researched, insightfully reasoned, and eloquently written paper, if it does not answer the assigned question, most instructors will find it unsatisfactory. Read the question carefully when you begin your work, reread it as you are doing any reading or research that may be required, reread it when you sit down to write, and reread it as you begin your final draft. People's minds, especially intelligent people's minds, have a tendency to drift to interesting and related, but not always pertinent, topics.

Even when the assignment is not presented as a question, you must formulate one to address in your paper. Three features distinguish a question that will serve as a strong foundation for a sociology paper. First, a helpful question reflects an understanding of sociology's distinctive perspective on human life. Second, it is carefully posed and framed. Third, it is asked in such a way that it lends itself to a logical and well-structured answer (in contrast to a question that suggests an endless list, such as "What are all the roles adopted by leaders?" or is too open-ended, such as "Why are people irrational?"). The following sections will help you to meet these three criteria for asking good questions.

What Is Sociology?

Failing to understand what sociology is and what sociologists do is a main reason that students experience difficulty in writing successful sociology papers. Since asking a good sociological question depends on understanding what sociology is, this section defines sociology and discusses how it is different from other fields.

Sociology is the study of human social behavior. Its basic insight is that human behavior is shaped by interaction among people. In other words, who a person is, what she or he thinks and does, is affected by the groups of which that person is a member. Sociologists investigate how individuals are shaped by their social groups, from families to nations, and how groups are created and maintained by the individuals who compose them.

Another part of sociology's insight is that interaction takes place in ways which are patterned, even though the people involved may be separated by many years or many miles or may appear to have differences. For example, societies at different historical times or in different geographical locations all find ways to enforce rules, to teach children valued beliefs, and to organize the production of goods necessary to their members' welfare. Sociologists try to understand the consistencies in these processes—the ways in which their similarities and differences follow a predictable pattern.

Sociology and Other Perspectives on Human Behavior

Sometimes new students (and more experienced ones!) are confused about how sociology is distinguished from other disciplines which study people, such as psychology, political science, history, philosophy, anthropology, or economics. In fact, these fields are not totally distinct. Sometimes the interests shared by different fields are easy to see, as with political sociology and political science, for example. But even when the overlap is less apparent, some theorists and researchers in each field share concerns and methods with those in neighboring disciplines.

Right now, however, we want to focus on what is distinctive about sociology because, in order to write successfully in any discipline, you need to have some idea of its boundaries. Our brief sketch necessarily simplifies the definitions of sociology and its "neighbors" and exaggerates their dissimilarities. The differences discussed below are intended primarily to sensitize you to sociology's distinctive features; they are not rigidly observed by theorists or researchers. In fact, many scholars describe themselves explicitly in terms that cross these boundaries (such as social historians, political economists, and social psychologists), often incorporating a sociological perspective into other disciplines.

The following summary compares and contrasts sociology with psychology, political science, history, philosophy, economics, and anthropology. We have illustrated their differences by showing how researchers in each field might approach one aspect of human life—deviant behavior.

Sociology and psychology

Similarities: Both are concerned with attitudes, beliefs, behavior, emotions, and interpersonal relationships.

Differences: Psychology is more likely to focus on the individual level of human behavior. When sociology considers the individual, it is within the context of social groups.

Studying deviance: Psychologists investigate the categories of mental disorders underlying deviant behavior. A sociologist might try to discover whether members of one socioeconomic class are more likely than members of another class to be labeled "mentally ill."

Sociology and political science

Similarities: Both are concerned with government.

Differences: Political scientists analyze different forms of government and their underlying philosophies and study the political process. A sociologist is more likely to examine the interrelationship between political structure and behavior and other aspects of society, such as the economy, religious institutions, and the attitudes of various social groups.

Studying deviance: A political scientist might analyze laws regulating deviance. A sociologist might examine how such laws change as the members of society adopt different ideological beliefs or how they serve the interests of some classes more than others.

Sociology and history

Similarities: Both look at human life over time.

Differences: Historians are more likely to focus on the influence of individuals and on the causes of specific events. Sociologists concentrate on the causes and effects of changes in patterns of social life, among both famous and ordinary people.

Studying deviance: A historian might interpret the motivations and actions of influential deviant individuals and attempt to explain their influence. A sociologist is more likely to trace changes in society's ways of defining and controlling deviant behavior.

Sociology and philosophy

Similarities: Both are interested in beliefs about the nature of life.

Differences: Philosophy is a system of abstract reasoning that follows specific rules of logic. Sociology is empirical: it seeks to discover information about the real world by gathering data about what people actually do.

Studying deviance: Philosophers might ask "What is good?" and "What is evil?" or analyze the appropriate uses of the term "deviance." Sociologists stick to what actually goes on in the social world, asking, for instance, "What do members of this particular society or subculture believe is 'right' and 'wrong'?"

Sociology and anthropology

Similarities: Both are concerned with social life, including culture, beliefs, decision making, relationships, and so on.

Differences: Anthropology is more likely to study societies other than our own, and to compare aspects of society cross-culturally.

Studying deviance: Anthropologists might travel to an isolated, nonindustrialized society to study how it defines and treats deviant behavior, or they might compare differences in rates of deviance in industrialized societies and nonindustrialized societies. Sociologists often study the same processes but are more likely to focus on a single society.

Sociology and economics

Similarities: Both are concerned with how society produces and distributes goods and services.

Differences: While an economist concentrates on the economy in its own right, sociologists are more likely to consider how the economy affects and is affected by other social processes.

Studying deviance: An economist might study the contributions and costs of deviance to the gross national product. A sociologist might study how the control of the economy by upper social classes provokes deviant behavior, such as burglary and theft, by those without access to a fair share of goods and services.

The Sociological Imagination

One way to describe what is distinctive about a sociological point of view is the "sociological imagination," a phrase coined by C. Wright Mills (1959). Using the sociological imagination means recognizing the connection between individual, private experience and the wider society. Mills calls the personal level an individual's "biography"; he uses the term "history" to refer to patterns and relationships on the larger scale of society. (As you can see, often it is sociologists who focus on what Mills calls "history," and historians who concentrate on what he refers to as "biography"!)

As a student, for example, you have followed your own life path to college. Being a college student is part of your personal life story. Your family has its own beliefs about what a college education means. You have your own academic and career goals. You have individual feelings and attitudes about the subjects covered in your classes and your own mixture of college and work schedules. All these things make up your personal, *biographical* experience of your life as a college student.

Applying sociological imagination to your college life expands your perspective. It is like a wide-angle lens that allows you to see yourself in a larger, more complex (and, in many ways, more interesting) picture. Using sociological imagination, you can begin to see where your experience as a college student fits into the social world in which you live, the *history* of which your biography is a part. Perhaps you are part of a trend among your peer group to major in computer science or communication studies. It could be that you are part of an ethnic group whose members are underrepresented in higher education. Perhaps your academic goals have been affected by social values (say, an increasing emphasis on the need for a college degree), or maybe your career choice, combined with many others', will affect the way society's work force is balanced between producing goods and providing services.

To use sociological imagination, then, is to identify the intersection of biography and history, the ways in which people are affected by social forces and social groups are affected by their members. As Mills (1959) himself put it,

> Every individual lives, from one generation to the next, in some society; . . . he [or she] lives out a biography, and . . . he lives it out with some historical sequence. By the fact of his living he contributes, however minutely, to the shaping of his society and its history; even as he is made by society and by its historical push and shove. (6)

Mills's deceptively simple insight—that people both affect their own destiny *and* are swept by currents of history—challenges and eludes sociologists from freshmen just starting to study the field to seasoned scholars. The key to using sociological imagination is to not lose sight of either side of this relationship.

Sociology's Focus and Methods

Like other disciplines, sociology has several major subdisciplines— variations on a theme, as it were. Some focus on large-scale "macro" phenomena such as political activities or economic relations. Some focus on "micro" activities which occur on a face-to-face basis such as in families, small groups, or work settings, or among friends. Like- wise, sociology may examine events which are as momentary as the eye contact between strangers on a bus or as long-term as the indus- trialization of society. It may deal with social life in terms of its struc- ture, attempting to uncover stable, underlying patterns, or it may look at the interactional processes through which individuals relate socially.

Sociology's methods vary considerably, but all are rooted in sci- ence. Basically, this means that sociologists systematically collect in- formation about the social world and then analyze this verifiable evidence, or data. The data may come from any of a number of sources—from controlled laboratory experiments, from written ac- counts of social life, or from observing, interviewing, or surveying people involved in the phenomenon being investigated. (In Part II of this book, we present tips on how you can use four different data sources, which represent the most typical sources on which under- graduate sociology papers are based.)

From their data, sociologists try to develop theories which explain what they observe. A theory is an explanation which the theorist claims can be generalized to all cases of the phenomenon under investigation. A strong theory must be supported by data.

The research process does not end with the proposal of a theory. Other researchers often use earlier theories to develop questions for other studies. In some instances they are trying to verify that the theory is correct—that the general explanation fits their own observations. At other times, they are challenging the validity of the theory because of differences between what they observe and what the theory suggests, and they want to offer an alternative explanation.

The question-and-answer process in sociological research follows one of two general patterns. It may be essentially *deductive* in nature: asking a question; using previously proposed theories to suggest an answer (or "hypothesis"); collecting and analyzing data to determine whether the hypothesis is accurate. Or it may be basically *inductive:* asking a question; collecting data; using the data to develop hypothesis in answer to the question. The main difference, obviously, is whether data are collected in order to test the hypothesis (deductive) or to create it (inductive).

One of the differences between high school and college is that in high school "learning" usually means learning facts. The students who demonstrate that they have learned the most facts earn the highest grades. In college, however, there is greater emphasis on analytical reasoning and thinking. Students are expected to comprehend entire systems of knowledge. Moreover, students find that there is often more than one correct way to approach a topic. That is, there is more than one *perspective* on an issue. A perspective is a way of looking at a topic. Think about looking at a house. If you look at it from the front, you see a door and windows with a roof overhead. If you look from the side you might see no doors, only windows. If you take the perspective from above, you see neither doors nor windows, only the roof. All three perspectives see the same house, but observers from the different perspectives would report very different descriptions. And all would be "correct."

Intellectual perspectives are like that. Earlier we noted that different disciplines have different perspectives on deviance. All look at the same behavior, but paint very different descriptions, and develop very different theories. Even *within* sociology there are several perspectives. Beginning students may find this confusing. For example, *conflict perspectives* and *consensus perspectives* look at society from the perspective of ever-present conflict or from the perspective of ever-present solidarity. *Microsociological perspectives* look from the point of view of everyday interaction among small groups of people, and *macrosociological perspectives* see things from the point of view of long-term change and societies as a whole.

To some extent these perspectives disagree about what the facts of society are, but more often than not they are asking different questions. It's like looking at the house from different perspectives. For example, the conflict perspective on deviance asks how some groups in society exercise the power to define other people's actions as deviant, focusing on how rules are made. Consensus sociologists might ask why some people break the rules, focusing on the individual deviant. A microsociologist might examine the process of becoming deviant from the deviant's point of view, while macrosociologists might ask how definitions of deviance have changed over the past few centuries. All of these perspectives share the features of sociology discussed above, but all ask different questions within the sociological framework.

Some students struggle with the cognitive ambiguity when different perspectives with very different implications exist and are accepted at the same time. In fact, this is one of the great intellectual feats of a college education, to be able to juggle more than one perspective in one's mind at the same time.

Sociology not only encompasses a wide range of approaches to research and theory; sociologists also apply those approaches to questions about an innumerable array of topics. In sociology classes you might study anything from the sociology of sports to the sociology of religion. You might learn about how those engaged in different occupations perceive their work lives, how a thief accomplishes her or his crime, or how children learn table manners. You might study birthrates, medical decision making, or the sex lives of teenagers in the 1930s as compared with the 1980s. For each of these subjects, there are sociologists who disagree about what kinds of questions should be asked and what methods should be used to answer them. Some sociology departments specialize in one topic or method. But usually they include faculty who represent a range of sociological concerns and styles. Course curricula, including writing assignments, reflect this variety, and students typically have the opportunity to become familiar with several ways of asking and answering sociological questions. When you are trying to understand what an assignment requires of you, it will help to keep in mind the focus of the course as a whole and the particular approach your instructor is presenting.

Sociology, then, is a diverse field. But, across all sociological methods and topics, a sociological perspective involves seeing individuals interacting as members of social groups. As you prepare to formulate the question that will underlie your sociology paper, remember that *adopting the sociological perspective is always the first step* in writing a successful paper.

Framing a Question

Writing a good sociology paper requires using your sociological imagination to frame an interesting question that then guides your research effort. Asking a sociologically imaginative question is one of the tasks students find most challenging and most difficult to pin down. There is no magic recipe, but here are some tips that might help. Your instructor may feel that some aspects of what we say are more important than others, so remember that these are just suggestions.

Remember the "history" part of the sociological imagination. Avoid overly individualistic or psychological questions, questions that concern only what happens inside a person's head. For example, asking whether criminals are motivated more by aggression than by greed is more interesting psychologically than sociologically. (We are in no way implying that psychological questions are inferior to sociological questions, but for our purposes here we are emphasizing the sociological aspects of human life.) A sociologically imaginative question might ask what aspects of social life—such as race, class, or gender—influence people to act out their aggression or greed in socially acceptable or unacceptable ways.

Remember the "biography" part of the sociological imagination. Avoid overly economic questions that drop people out of the picture. (Again, economic questions are often interesting and important, but we want to emphasize the sociological aspects.) For example, asking how much income is lost to crime each year is less sociologically imaginative than asking what types of crime typically victimize wealthy people as compared to poor people.

Ask a question concerning *differences* between individuals, groups, roles, relationships, societies, or time periods. Only rarely do sociologists make claims about all people or all societies. They are typically more interested in how and why people or societies differ from each other; that is, they more frequently ask questions about variation than about uniformity. For example, they would probably not ask whether people are by nature aggressive but rather why some people are more aggressive than others. Are highly aggressive people socialized differently, part of a different subculture, vulnerable to different social pressures, or aspiring to different goals than less aggressive people?

The remaining four suggestions apply to questions for any discipline, not just sociology.

Ask a question that has more than one plausible answer. The paper's task is to demonstrate why your answer is more valid than other plausible answers. You must argue why your answer is more correct and convincing than alternative answers. It wastes both your time and your reader's to belabor the obvious. For example, whether there is widespread public opinion against violent crime can only have one plausible answer. No one would seriously claim otherwise. Before starting the research, specify different plausible answers to your question. Can you imagine anyone seriously taking the other side? If not, you need to reformulate the question.

Unless your assignment specifies otherwise, ask a question that draws relationships between two or more concepts. (Some exceptions are a definition paper, a "feeling" or reaction paper, a story or narrative paper.) Typically, assigned questions concern the relationship between concepts. Are two concepts (for example, deviance and socialization) empirically associated or not? That is, are deviants likely to be socialized differently from nondeviants? Are two concepts (for example, social prestige and deviance) negatively associated, that is, when one is high, is the other low? For example, are people with high prestige less likely to engage in crime than people with low prestige? Unless specifically instructed, avoid questions that address only one concept, such as "What is deviance?"

Make sure you have access to the information to answer your question. Although some paper assignments do not require any research outside assigned readings and lectures, many do require you to document your points with evidence. For these papers, you must consider when you ask your question whether you can realistically get the necessary documentation. For example, "Has deviance always existed?" is an interesting question with important consequences for sociological theory. But it would be difficult to document adequately whether prehistoric societies had deviance or not. On the other hand, students are sometimes surprised to discover what information does exist and can be tracked down with a little work, so it is best to check with your instructor if you are unsure.

Make sure your question is answerable in the space allowed. This may be the most elusive of our tips and the one students falter on most frequently. Part of the difficulty is that some instructors expect finer detail of documentation or a more fully developed argument than others. Another problem is that students often don't know how much information they will find until they have done their research. Here are two guidelines. First, ask "middle range" questions that are neither grand, monumental, deep truth questions nor minutely exacting, picky detail questions. Second, check out your question with your instructor before you begin your research.

To sum up this section, then, we want to stress that a good paper should not just be *about* some topic (like mental health, race, gender, or occupations). For example, rather than a paper about social mobility, you might frame and address the question "Is there more opportunity for upward mobility in America today than a hundred years ago?" Notice that this question concerns differences between two fairly specific time periods. And it has more than one plausible answer; reasonable people could disagree about whether there is now more opportunity for mobility or less. Framing an answerable but debatable question is a fundamental, and sometimes the most demanding, part of writing a paper.

Terms and Strategies in Essay Assignments

When they are given a paper assignment, students naturally want to know what the instructor wants, but asking "What do you want us to do on this assignment?" usually annoys the instructor. From the instructor's point of view, the instructions already indicate what students are expected to do with the information. Knowing the course content is not enough to do well on a paper assignment; knowing *what to do* with this content, in other words, having a strategy for selecting and presenting this information, is essential. The way to determine such an appropriate strategy is to scrutinize the wording of assignments, to clarify for yourself what is expected, and then to use a suitable strategy to produce the paper.

Instructors deliberately design assignments to get you to work with—and think about—course concepts and data in various ways. For example, writing about deviance could involve defining it, illustrating it, analyzing it, comparing it to other behavior, evaluating its effects, summarizing someone's theories about it, etc. Sometimes instructors will provide you with a well-framed, unambiguous question to start with. At the other extreme, you may be given a very vague assignment (like "Discuss deviance") which will require you to create and frame your own question. In the middle of this range are a common series of commands, illustrated below, which cue you to appropriate questions that can be framed concerning the course information and which tell you what the instructor wants you to do with this information.

Note that sometimes an assignment calls for more than one question because the instructor has deliberately combined these commands, thereby requiring you to work with the material in several ways, applying several different strategies. At other times instructors provide several different versions of essentially the same question but repeat it in different words to help you understand what you are supposed to do. If your assignment seems to call for several questions, first determine if they are the same single question in different words or if they involve separate strategies.

Analyze: Break something down into its parts, for example, a theory into its components, a process into its stages, an event into its causes. Analysis involves characterizing the whole, identifying the parts, and showing how the parts relate to each other to make the whole. Corresponding question: "What is the relationship between anomie and frustration in the functionalist theory of deviance?"

Assess / Criticize / Evaluate: Determine the importance or value of something. Assessing requires you to develop clearly stated criteria of judgment and to comment on the elements that meet or fail to meet those criteria. Corresponding question: "How useful is labeling theory for explaining why people join gangs?"

Classify: Sort something into main categories and thereby pidgeonhole its parts. Corresponding question: "If someone cheats on an examination to get a better grade, which of Merton's forms of deviance does the behavior belong to?"

Compare / Contrast: Identify the important similarities and differences between two elements in order to reveal something significant about them. Emphasize similarities if the command is to compare, and differences if it is to contrast. Corresponding question: "What are the similarities and differences in labeling theory and functionalist theories of deviance?"

Define / Identify: Give the special characteristics by which a concept, thing, or event can be recognized, that is, what it is and what it is not. Place it in its general class and then differentiate it from other members of that class. Corresponding questions: "What is anomie? What behaviors or attitudes indicate that a person or group is anomic?"

Describe: Present the characteristics by which an object, action, person, or concept can be recognized or an event or process can be visualized. Corresponding question: "What is Durkheim's theory of deviance?"

Discuss / Examine: You are given room to analyze, and/or evaluate a particular topic. You must decide on your own question concerning the things to be discussed. Instructors usually expect you to go beyond summary. Corresponding question: "What can sociological theories tell us about why gangs exist and why individuals join them?"

List / Enumerate: Give essential points one by one in a logical order. Corresponding question: "What are the forms of deviance in Merton's theory of deviance?"

Interpret: Explain what the author of a quotation means (not what you mean). Corresponding question: "What does Durkheim mean by stating that animals cannot commit suicide?"

Explain / Justify: Make clear the reasons for, or the basic principles of something; make it intelligible. Explanation may involve relating the unfamiliar to the more familiar. Corresponding questions: "Why do people break rules that they believe in? What theories do you think give the best explanation of this kind of behavior? What evidence can you present to support this theory?"

Illustrate: Use a concrete example to explain or clarify the essential attributes of a problem or concept. Corresponding question: "Give a concrete example of 'innovative deviance.' How does this example show the defining features of the concept?"

Outline / Trace / Review / State: Organize a description under main points and subordinate points, omitting minor details and stressing the classification of the elements of the problem or the main points in the development of an event or issue. Corresponding questions: "What have been the major debates over deviance in the past quarter century? How has the resolution of one debate led into the next? Highlight these debates with reference to leading theories and path-breaking studies."

Prove / Validate: Establish that something is true by citing factual evidence or giving clear, logical reasons for believing it is true. Corresponding question: "Make a case on behalf of or opposed to labeling theory. What are the strongest justification and best evidence you can present to support your point of view?"

Developing an Argument: Logic and Structure

Logic in writing refers to the relationship between the paper's assertions and its evidence. Structure concerns how the parts of the paper fit together. Sentences are the "trees" of the paper; logic and structure are the "forest." According to one faculty survey, structure and logic are among the most important criteria instructors weigh in grading papers.

Logic demands that a good paper go beyond mere assertion ("This statement is true because I say it is"). The answer to your question, which is your thesis, must be supported by evidence and reasoning. One way to accomplish this is to assume that the reader is naive (a Martian, for example) or skeptical. Try to imagine actively what a naive reader might not understand about what you are saying and explain your points to her or him. Try to imagine the kinds of doubts a skeptic might hold and attempt to convince her or him, just like a debater would.

Structure demands that in a good paper not only should each sentence be well written and make sense; it should also be logically connected to the sentences around it, each paragraph to the paragraphs around it, each section to the sections around it, and all of them to the overall theme of the paper. Whether you write sentence by sentence or begin with a general plan and work down to the level of the sentence, by the time you hand the paper in, you should be able to conceptualize the structure of the whole paper in your head (and, if necessary, to explain that structure to the instructor). This means being able to say in one or two sentences what the paper's main thesis is and how you go about arguing that thesis. Imagine your roommate or a friend asking "What's the point of the paper?" and "Why should the reader believe you?" If you can't answer those questions, you still have work to do before turning in the final draft.

The next step after framing your question is constructing a logical defense of your thesis—why your answer is more correct than alternative answers. This defense requires pieces of evidence that support your thesis. The evidence must be logically connected to the thesis so that you can make the statement (either in your head or in the paper) "If the evidence is true, the thesis is true." Many student papers (and some professional papers) falter here, presenting interesting and important evidence in narrative form, or in a controlled study, or sometimes through reasoned reflection, but then drawing a conclusion that is less than warranted by the evidence presented. So be sure to put aside the actual paper and think through the first three items on the checklist presented in Chapter 10: "What is my thesis? Does my thesis remain evident and central throughout the paper? Have I supported my thesis with adequate evidence?"

Finally, the structure of the paper should reflect the logical connection of the evidence to the thesis. It is the writer's job, not the reader's, to draw the connections between evidence and conclusions and to show how the paper logically proceeds. Thus the paper's introduction, transitions, and conclusions are essential, not just incidental parts of the paper. The *introduction* should state the question that is being answered and specify the plan for answering it. As the paper unfolds, provide guideposts for the reader telling where the paper has gone and where it is going. These *transitions* indicate how sentences, paragraphs, and sections logically fit together. Transitions can be accomplished by phrases like "On the other hand" or single words like "Furthermore." (See Chapter 10 for a list of transitions.) Or they can be stated in sentences like "The last section discussed Durkheim's basic presuppositions; this section will show how those presuppositions influenced his theory of religion." A common writing error is the *nonsequitur*, a Latin phrase for sentences or paragraphs that have no apparent connection. They often result from a connection that is in the writer's mind but which she or he fails to demonstrate to the reader. A *conclusion* should remind readers where they have been and why you think the thesis has been demonstrated. Try to summarize the paper without repeating specific sentences. This is also the appropriate place to reflect upon the larger implications of your thesis—to answer the question "So what?" But it is not appropriate to present new evidence in the conclusion.

Two Formats of Logic and Structure

We suggest here two formats of logic and structure that are common in sociology papers. There are, of course, other formats which may be appropriate for specific assignments. If the paper assignment does not specify an explicit format requirement, it is often helpful to talk over your format ideas with the instructor.

The "Three-Part Essay" Format This type of paper is most commonly structured in terms of a major thesis (which answers a question) and three supporting "points."

There is nothing magical about the number three; it is a convenient number of points for the length and scope of papers typically written for course assignments. Each of the three points should logically support the thesis. You should be able to say "If point A (or B, or C) is true, the thesis is true." More precisely in terms of formal logic, you need to be able to maintain that "if point A (or B, or C) were *not* true, the thesis would probably not be true."

Take as an example the thesis "Over the last hundred years, educational opportunities in America have opened up the American social structure to more upward mobility."

Point A could be: Educational achievement is more closely connected to high-status jobs than it was a hundred years ago.

Point B could be: Education is more equally accessible to all members of the society than were earlier means of determining people's status.

Point C could be: The content of education relates more to job skills than it did a hundred years ago.

The paper itself is structured around an introduction, discussion of point A, discussion of point B, discussion of point C, and conclusion. The introduction presents the question that is being answered, the general thesis, and usually a plan of the body of the paper. Each point is discussed in turn. Each section usually starts with a claim—a statement of its main point. Often the next sentence is an example of this claim, followed by an explanation of how the example illustrates the point. Then you can elaborate on this point, identify its implications, take issue with some aspects, or provide other types of evidence. Finally, you need to tie it back in with your general thesis and with the argument so far.

You will need at least one paragraph for each discussion section, because that's what a paragraph is—a logical section with one main point. You may need more than one paragraph to deal with each main point, especially if the point is complicated or if you are presenting elaborate evidence. If you do, allocate separate paragraphs to each subpoint or aspect. This often happens when you want to analyze a particularly revealing example and explain to what extent it does, but also does *not*, illustrate a point you want to make. In other words, the discussion gives evidence and reasoning for why the point is true; the discussion also explains the logical connection between that point and the general thesis.

The conclusion then summarizes the overall argument and often offers your personal thoughts about the issue you have discussed.

A modified version of the essay format is also appropriate for a paper based on ethnographic research. If that is the kind of paper you're preparing, follow the structure described in this section, replacing the thesis and supporting claims with three major themes, or three points about a single theme, gleaned from your data. See Chapter 8 for details on this modified application.

The "Journal" Format   This is the format often found in articles in major academic journals such as the *American Sociological Review* or the *American Journal of Sociology*. The journal format is not the same as "journalistic style." The term "journalistic style" is sometimes used to describe the easy and fluid style of writing in popular magazines like *Time*, *Newsweek*, or *Life*. The journal format refers to a particular way that a paper or article can be organized. One would almost never use the journalistic style of writing in a paper organized according to the journal format. The journal format follows the procedural logic of the "hypothesis testing" mode of conducting research, in which you formally test a specific hypothesis through systematic research. The journal format, although usable for projects other than formal hypothesis testing, is best suited to projects that include some sort of systematic data collection and analysis. Its structure follows this order: Introduction (including the literature review and the statement of hypothesis), Methods, Results, and Discussion. (See Chapter 9 on the quantitative research paper for more detail.)

The Introduction specifies the question that is being answered in your paper and your general thesis. In this section, a "review of the literature" summarizes what other people have written about the topic, explaining why it is an important issue to study and what their answers are. This section should also formally state your hypothesis (for example, "A greater proportion of men today hold higher-status jobs than their fathers did a hundred years ago") and justify why you expect it to be true.

The Methods section reports your research procedure, detailing where you got the data, how the variables were measured, and what sort of analysis you conducted on the data. A reader should be able to replicate your study by following the "cookbook" of your methods section.

The Results section reports in literal terms what the study shows. For instance, "30 percent of men a hundred years ago were in higher-status jobs than their fathers, while 29 percent of men today are in higher-status jobs than their fathers," which is virtually no change. (These numbers are made up for this book. They are not accurate.)

The Discussion section draws the conclusions and reflects upon the result—for example: "The hypothesis must be rejected. The occupational structure has not opened up. The American promise of an equal chance for all is not yet fulfilled."

The essay and journal formats are illustrated by sample student papers in this book. The paper on quantitative research (Chapter 9) follows the journal format. The remaining two sample papers—one based on ethnographic field research (Chapter 8) and one demonstrating a textual analysis (Chapter 6)—are modified versions of the essay format. See the relevant chapters for details on organizing your paper.

Chapter 2

ORGANIZING YOUR TIME: THE TIME GRID

It's worth repeating: half the battle is won when the first word is written. You wouldn't believe the wild contortions professional writers go through to avoid writing that first word of the day. Pencils must be sharpened; typewriters cleaned and ribbons changed; filing demands to be done; the cat must be let out; that filthy window must be cleaned; shelves of books must be rearranged; a letter must be mailed; the cat must be let back in.

GENE OLSON,
Sweet Agony: A Writing Manual of Sorts

Here is a tool to get you started—a semester/quarter time grid (See Figure 2–1). The first stage of the writing process can be agonizing for many people. We believe that the key to writing better papers, with less anxiety, is starting early enough to write more than one draft. Many students experience "writer's block" because they think they should be able to produce a finished product on the first try. Paper writing, therefore, seems nearly impossible and is put off until the night before the due date. Then, because writing done at the last minute is often inadequate, the students' doubts about themselves as writers are confirmed. Some students move in a vicious cycle of anxiety, procrastination, and, almost inevitably, disappointing results. A time grid can help you break this pattern and feel more in control of the writing process.

By looking at the whole semester or quarter, you can set up a realistic plan for completing your paper, taking into consideration your exams, other assignments, and other commitments. (We suggest photocopying a hand-drawn, blank time grid so that you can write on it easily and reuse it every semester or quarter.) Filling in the time grid will pay the following dividends: it forces you to break up what may loom as an enormous task—writing a whole paper in one sitting—into smaller, "do-able" tasks. When you set a beginning date for each small task, you will probably get started sooner and avoid the guilt and anxiety that often accompany procrastination. Moreover, this approach to writing usually results in your learning more and earning a higher grade because you have allowed time for all the steps in the process of preparing a good paper.

Some papers are assigned early in the semester or quarter and are not due until the end, while others are assigned only a few weeks before the due date. Although the time grid is most helpful when you have most of the semester to complete your paper, our advice on organizing your time applies to short-term papers as well. Even when you have only a few weeks to complete your paper assignment, planning will pay off. Planning involves two steps: first, determining your specific writing tasks; and, second, appropriately allocating your time among these tasks.

To set up a work schedule, you must first determine your tasks. For illustration we will use the four most typical kinds of papers assigned in sociology classes: textual analysis, library research, ethnographic field research, and quantitative research. These kinds of papers are discussed in Part II.

The first task for all types of papers is choosing a topic, unless, of course, a topic is assigned. Select a provisional topic as early as possible, because it will probably evolve as you find references and become more familiar with the readings or the field setting. You can never know if a possible topic for a library or quantitative paper will work out until you at least skim some possible sources. Nor can you decide on a topic for an ethnographic field research paper until you get permission to visit the setting and observe the people there.

Except for topic selection, the four types of papers involve different tasks and therefore different ways of setting up a work schedule. As you can see from Table 2–1, each type of paper requires a different set of tasks to be completed in a certain order. Study this table carefully. As you can see, the beginning and concluding stages of all papers are the same; they all involve selecting a topic, framing an appropriate question, and writing drafts, ideally three drafts (two rough and a final one to turn in). However, each paper has different middle steps: a quantitative paper has seven different middle tasks; an ethnographic field research paper has five; a textual analysis has only two; a library research paper has three. The way you allocate your time, then, depends on the type of paper you are writing.

Your paper schedule will also vary according to the length of your semester or quarter and the time between assignment and due date.

Table 2–1 Determining Your Tasks

	Textual	Library	Ethno-graphic Field	Quanti-tative
Pick and narrow down your topic; frame an appropriate question; verify with your instructor	X	X	X	X
Different middle steps:				
Locate references in the library		X	—[a]	X
Take notes on library references		X	—[a]	X
Take notes for analysis of text(s)	X			
Write a provisional thesis and outline; consult your instructor	X	X		X
Write a plan for data collection and analysis; consult instructor			X	X
Construct data collection instruments, design methods, etc.				X
Collect data			X	X
Analyze data			X	X
Write a rough draft; type draft 1 (and print out, if applicable)	X	X	X	X
Revise; then type draft 2 (and print out, if applicable)	X	X	X	X
Revise, partly by going over the "Checklist for Polishing" (Chapter 10)	X	X	X	X
Read "Guidelines for Typing and Submitting Your Paper" (Chapter 11); type final copy (and print out, if applicable)	X	X	X	X
Proofread, correct, and photocopy	X	X	X	X

[a] These steps are not required of all ethnographic field research papers. You should check with your instructor to determine whether your assignment requires these two steps.

Therefore, we can suggest only *general guidelines* for scheduling your time. Once you have selected your topic, we estimate that you should spend approximately 50–70 percent of your time completing the middle steps required for your type of paper. The remaining 30–50 percent of your time should be spent completing the last five steps— from writing your first rough draft to photocopying your final draft—

with the majority of that time spent on revising. In Table 2–2 we estimate, for each type of paper, how you should allocate your time among the required tasks.

On the basis of Table 2–2, we can compare and contrast the allocation of time for each type of paper (assuming that the level of difficulty and time allowed for writing do not vary significantly). For a library paper, you will spend much of your time gathering references and taking notes on them. For a textual analysis, you will also spend much of your time reading and taking notes, but you will concentrate on only one or two texts. When you write an ethnographic field research paper, you will spend less time reading references and more time collecting data and recording notes. A quantitative paper requires a combination of tasks. You will devote about a third of your time to library research, another third to designing your study and collecting and analyzing your data, and only the last third to writing your paper. (This description of tasks is simplified; for necessary details about each type of paper see the appropriate chapter in Part II.)

Now you are ready to work with the time grid. Begin by filling in the name of the month in the first column and the dates in the small boxes (inside the larger boxes). If the month changes in the middle of the week, do not skip down to the next row. Just continue the dates for the new month in the very next box, and go back and label the new month in the first column.

The time grid should be long enough to accommodate a 20-week semester. If you are on a shorter semester (15–18 weeks) or quarter system (10 weeks), simply cross out the weeks your college is not in session. Once all the dates are filled in, write in the exams, quizzes,

Table 2–2   Allocating Your Time

	Textual	Library	Field	Quanti-tative
Select topic and references	10%	20%	10%	10%
Read and take notes (including the writing of a provisional thesis, outline, and method plan, if applicable)	40	30	10	30
Collect and analyze data (including the construction of data collection instruments, if applicable)			50	30
Writing, revising, and polishing	50	50	30	30
Total time	100	100	100	100

and major assignments from all your classes in the larger boxes corresponding to their due dates. Include any other important deadlines or events that may influence your writing schedule, whether school related or not.

Next, choose a date on the time grid when you will begin each required task listed in Table 2–1 for your type of paper. Write the task in pencil in the large box corresponding to that date. So as not to clutter up the grid, make the beginning dates of new tasks also represent completion deadlines for the previous task. Apportion your time according to Table 2–2. For example, if you are on the quarter system, and at the beginning of the quarter your instructor assigns a quantitative paper to be due at the end of the quarter, you will have a maximum of 9–10 weeks to complete your paper after selecting a topic. Therefore, on your time grid you will divide the first 5–6 weeks of the quarter into days for completing the middle steps of the writing process, and the last 3–4 weeks into days for writing, revising, and polishing your paper. (Figure 2–1 gives a sample time grid for a quantitative paper written during a 10-week quarter.) No matter what type of paper you are writing or how much time you have from assignment to due date, be sure to mark off enough time on your time grid to write and/or revise more than one draft. It is also advisable to build your schedule so that it ends *before* the absolute deadline, since unexpected events may keep you from meeting the due date.

As soon as you have selected a topic and framed your question, discuss it with your instructor. Soon afterward show him or her a written thesis, outline, and/or plan for data collection and analysis (if applicable). Thirty minutes with your instructor will lessen anxiety

The Night Before the Deadline

during the remainder of the writing process, which is not a bad trade-off. (You are more likely to get 30 uninterrupted minutes with your instructor if you make an appointment rather than pop in during office hours.)

The semester/quarter time grid will work only if you stick to it. Put it in a prominent place (e.g., taped to a mirror or refrigerator) so you will see it every day. Many students find that the time grid not only helps them produce better papers but also keeps them on top of their other assignments.

Figure 2–1 Sample Time Grid for a Quantitative

Week	Month	Sunday		Monday		Tuesday	
Week 1	Oct.				3		4		5
Week 2		Pick & Narrow Down Topic & Frame Question	10	Verify Topic & Question w. Professor; Locate References	11	MATH QUIZ	12
Week 3		Start Reading & Note taking	17		18		19
Week 4			24	Write Provisional thesis, outline & methods plan; verify with Prof.	25	MATH QUIZ	26
Week 5	Nov.		31		1		2
Week 6		Begin Data Analysis	7		8	MATH QUIZ	9
Week 7		Begin Writing 1st Rough Draft	14		15		16
Week 8			21		22	MATH QUIZ	23
Week 9	Dec.	Begin Revisions of Draft 2 (checklist for polishing)	28		29		30
Week 10			5		6	MATH QUIZ proofread, correct, & photocopy	7

Make an appointment with your instructor.

Although the month changed, stay on the same line of the time grid. Mark the new month in the first column.

Begin your writing early to allow time for revising.

Revise partly by going over the "Checklist for Polishing," Chapter 10.

Allow time for proofreading, correcting, and photocopying your paper.

* We have used the quantitative paper for our sample time grid because it has the most steps. Your time grid may have fewer boxes filled in than the one above.

Paper Written During a 10-Week Quarter*

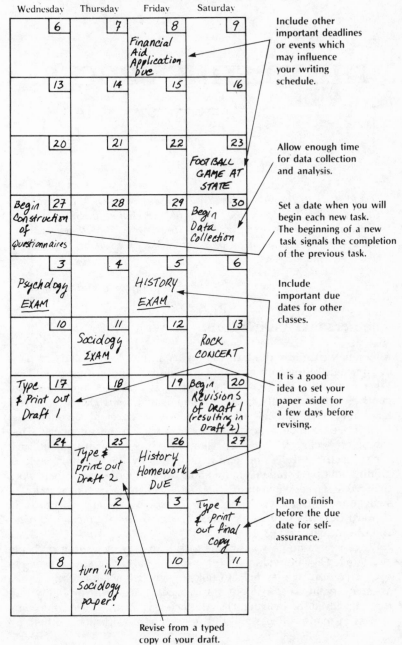

Wednesday Thursday Friday Saturday

6 **7** **8** **9**
Financial Aid Application Due

Include other important deadlines or events which may influence your writing schedule.

13 **14** **15** **16**

20 **21** **22** **23**
FOOTBALL GAME AT STATE

Allow enough time for data collection and analysis.

27 Begin Construction of Questionnaires **28** **29** **30** Begin Data Collection

Set a date when you will begin each new task. The beginning of a new task signals the completion of the previous task.

3 Psychology EXAM **4** **5** HISTORY EXAM **6**

Include important due dates for other classes.

10 **11** Sociology EXAM **12** **13** ROCK CONCERT

17 Type & Print out Draft 1 **18** **19** Begin Revisions of Draft 1 (resulting in Draft 2) **20**

It is a good idea to set your paper aside for a few days before revising.

24 **25** Type & print out Draft 2 **26** History Homework DUE **27**

1 **2** **3** **4** Type & print out final Copy

Plan to finish before the due date for self-assurance.

8 **9** turn in Sociology paper! **10** **11**

Revise from a typed copy of your draft.

Chapter 3

THE WRITING PROCESS

I told students that it didn't make much difference what they wrote in a first draft because they could always change it. Since what they put on a piece of paper was not necessarily final, they needn't worry so much about what they wrote. The only version that mattered was the last one.

HOWARD S. BECKER
Writing for Social Scientists

The Personal Vulnerability of Writing

Although we usually think of writing as an intellectual activity, a lot of personal feelings are at stake, especially when writing in college. When you write for a class, the writing is evaluated and most students feel that *they* are being evaluated, that somebody they barely know and have not had the opportunity to develop personal trust with is telling them whether they are worthy to be in college. That can be very scary. It's not surprising that students want to avoid such a risky activity. It is not made any easier by the common style of grading that tells students more about what is wrong with their work than what is good about it. (For an excellent personal account of struggling with these feelings see "Risk" by Pamela Richards in Howard Becker's *Writing for Social Scientists* (1984. Chicago: University of Chicago Press).

We can offer no easy solutions to the anxiety of writing or being evaluated. Few individuals, even professional writers, are ever entirely free of it. It may help to talk to your fellow students, teaching assistant, or instructor about your concerns. You will probably find that they (even the instructor) share the same feelings. The counseling centers at many colleges and universities have workshops to help alleviate your anxieties. In extreme cases, where "writer's block" prevents you from completing assignments or hurts the quality of your work, professional counseling may be appropriate.

Here are a few insights we can offer.

Different people have very different ways of composing a first draft. Some need to sharpen two pencils and make a cup of coffee; some can only write in the morning, others late at night; some can only type and others compose only in longhand. One of the authors of this book writes best while shoeless! None of these things matter, as long as the writing gets done. Students sometimes feel that there is a correct way to go about sitting down to write and that any personal quirks should be "cured." But they forget that writing can be an emotionally risky venture and that people often need little rituals to ease the tension. Just like the basketball player who caresses the basketball before shooting a foul shot, the baseball player who always knocks the mud off his shoes before stepping into the batter's box, or the ballerina who sits in the middle of the stage for five minutes before the curtain goes up, anything (provided it's legal and nondestructive) necessary to get ready for writing is appropriate as long as you don't do it *instead* of writing.

The secret to writing is rewriting. No one ever sits down and writes an excellent paper at one go. Believing that myth is a major cause of writer's block and anxiety about writing. Writing is definitely *not* a delivery system of ready-made ideas; it is a process of approximation. A writer works by getting something down on paper—doodles, an outline, a provisional question or list of questions, a draft, or whatever—looks at it, likes some aspects and considers a way to develop those, dislikes some other aspects and thinks about ways to change them, and in so doing gets more ideas to jot down, and so the process continues.

The expression of ideas on paper necessarily goes through stages. But there is no One Right Way or One Right Direction to move through these stages. For example, some people like to begin by writing down everything that occurs to them in association with the general topic; they may even turn off their computer monitor and simply keyboard in everything they can think of. They then print this out, search through it for threads of thought and rich possibilities, and then outline some sequence of the previously jumbled, buried ideas. Other writers work out a highly structured outline first because the logical subdivisions help them spot and understand potential relationships between ideas. Then they compose a draft, possibly beginning to write sentences and paragraphs about ideas somewhere in the middle or at the end of their outline. This is the way that student Alvin Hasegawa (see his paper in Chapter 9) works. He recommends outlining before the first rough draft: "The only advice I can give to another student is to start writing the paper with an outline. An outline guides the direction of the paper, it lets you get down something concrete to work with, and it gives you an idea of what you have to do." However, we've said that the very act of writing triggers thought, so you may find that outlining comes more easily after you've written some ideas or after your first rough draft.

We therefore are not recommending any one particular way to move through this writing and rewriting process. However, we would like to share with you some suggestions about stages in it—particularly the value of outlining and revising, and about the nature of writing style.

Outlining

Writing an outline can provide at least two benefits at different stages in the writing process: it can give birth to ideas and it can describe the connections between ideas that are already articulated. The first kind of outline is glorified doodling; the second kind of outline is a blueprint or a road map that tracks the relationship and sequence of main ideas in your paper. The first kind, to use C. Wright Mill's distinction (in *The Sociological Imagination*), is private; its purpose is discovery, not presentation to others. The second kind can very usefully be shown to an instructor long before the paper's due date, to make sure you're on target. It is much easier to revise this second kind of outline (add, omit, or shift main parts) than to repair a completed paper.

Discovery Outlines (private, just for your eyes)

1. **Freewriting.** This is brainstorming or free association. Just write from 5–15 minutes nonstop with no censoring of your ideas. If you are keyboarding on a computer, dim the screen so you're not distracted, and at the end of 15 minutes scroll back to find some key words or phrases you like, underline them, and then immediately use the "Insert" command to add 5–10 more minutes' worth of thoughts.

2. **Lists.** Make up a shopping list of all the ideas or questions that you can think of that you associate with or might need in any way for your paper, just as if you were going to the store for groceries. Then group them into families. This is easy to do on a computer with the "Move" and "Indent" commands.

3. **Reporter's Notebook.** Consider the famous journalism questions "Who?" "When?" "Why?" "Where?" "What?" and "How?," and try to create information related to the general topic for each question.

4. **Diagrams.** Some people are visually oriented and like to see their ideas emerging as pictures on the page. Here are several different kinds of diagrams:

- *Clustering.* Write one key word or phrase (for example, person's name, issue, term) in the middle of a sheet of paper. Circle it and then write down related concepts and examples in their own circles elsewhere on the page. Draw lines between the circles to indicate various logical relationships between all these items.
- *Branching.* Build a tree from a key word or phrase. Analyze it into its branch ideas and then into the twig and leaf ideas. Your tree can be vertical, horizontal, or upside down.
- *Columns.* Set up a compare/contrast table in two columns. Include in each column the information that fits under the things you are juxtaposing.

A computer tip. Computer programs exist for outlining ideas, e.g., MORE II and ACTA for the Macintosh. Even some word processing programs, like Microsoft Word, have outlining capabilities. Your own word processor may have such an outlining function. If so, learn how to use it. If not, use the "Indent" command to create, copy, and save an outline. You may want to use it later to begin drafting your paper by inserting material. In any case, most writers move back and forth between their outline and rough draft as work on one modifies the other.

Presentation Outlines (public, to show to others)

This is a completed set of ideas, arranged in a specific sequence. As such it's a map or blueprint to the paper itself. It can be a topic outline composed of words and phrases like a table of contents, or it can be a sentence outline. In either case, a proper presentation outline signals the order and relationship of ideas through visual layout (headings and indentations) and through a symbol system, either an alternating number-letter system (Roman numeral, capital letter, Arabic numeral, lowercase letter) or a number system, e.g., 1, 1.1, 1.1.2, etc.

Revising

Revising includes inserting new ideas and deleting or modifying old ones; rewriting sentences or paragraphs to improve clarity or logic; moving sentences or paragraphs around to strengthen organization; and adding transitions to enhance the flow of your paper and accentuate the relationships among your ideas. Revising can greatly improve the logic and structure of your argument, features of your paper explained in Chapter 1. Toward the end of the writing process, edit your paper by paying attention to mechanical matters such as punctuation and spelling. Setting your drafts aside for a few days between revisions helps you see their strengths and weaknesses more clearly.

Since revision can best be conducted from typed copies of your drafts, typing also aids your writing. You should type at least one draft before typing the copy you turn in, since problems such as lack of organization and clarity are more apparent in a typed draft. As one writing expert put it:

> The typewriter distances prose and it does it quickly. By depersonalizing our priceless prose, a typescript shows it to us as seen through a stranger's eyes. It tells us what it looks like, literally how it "shapes up." No single bad writing habit is so powerful as the habit of typing an essay only when you are ready to turn it in. Correct the handwritten manuscript by all means, but then type a draft and revise that. . . . The typed draft represents the central mechanical stage in the creative oscillation we go through, that back-and-forth movement in which first we suggest things to the prose and then it suggests things to us. (Lanham, 1979:54)

With a typed copy of your draft you can more easily use the "cut and paste" method of revision, which involves typing a rough draft and then cutting it up and putting it back together in a more logical order, leaving out sentences or paragraphs, or adding new ones. But we caution you to cut up a photocopy of the typed draft rather than the original, since you will probably want to refer to the original.

For the reasons given above, writers who lack typing skill are at a disadvantage, not only in college but also in many jobs. If you cannot type at least moderately well, perhaps you should investigate typing classes in your community; and, although you have little choice but longhand for the writing process, arrange well in advance of the due date to have the final draft typed by a skilled typist. Too many typographical errors (typos) blemish even an otherwise excellent paper.

Typing and revising are easier on a word processor or personal computer. With a computer you can quickly correct typos, move sentences and paragraphs around, and easily produce typed copies of your various drafts. We caution you to carefully proofread your final copy so that it doesn't contain words or phrases from former drafts you meant to delete.

Sandra Ducoff Garber, a student whose paper appears in Chapter 8, enthusiastically recommends word processing: "Using a computer was an immense help. The computer facilitated my style. Its editing capabilities were liberating. Because editing was easier than it would have been with a typewriter, I was more willing to edit the paper over and over again." Learning word processing is not difficult or excessively time-consuming, even for those who have had no prior experience with computers. You can also use word processing skills to write papers for other courses and, perhaps, in a future (or even current) job. Increasingly, colleges are establishing centers on campus where you can arrange to use a computer for course assignments. Find out whether your college has such a center.

We are not recommending that you *compose* your drafts in any particular way. Writing habits vary—some writers prefer to compose in longhand, others at a typewriter, and still others at a word processor. However, to repeat, we strongly recommend revising from a typed copy. (Be sure to print out the copy if you have typed your paper on a computer.) If you compose rough drafts in longhand, next type them, double-spacing and leaving ample margins (don't worry about typing perfectly, since these copies don't go to the instructor). Then revise. The revisions you make right on the typed copy should probably be in pencil, so you can erase if necessary. The limited area on the draft available for revising (margins and spaces between lines) gets depleted quickly if most of it gets blotched from ink that has been scribbled over; your revised drafts might become illegible, difficult to work with and to retype. (Long insertions, which require another piece of paper anyway, can be written in ink.)

When revising, think carefully about your paper's key concepts and terms. Define them as you introduce them (usually in the opening paragraphs) and use them accurately throughout the paper. Be especially cautious when using terms originated by sociologists that have become part of everyday language and yet retain special sociological meanings (e.g., "stereotype," "status," "self-fulfilling prophecy"). It's often helpful to write out sociological definitions of your central terms on scratch paper—in language you can understand—in order to foster clear and accurate use of them as you revise.

Finally, it's a good idea to locate a manual of style—which presents standards and examples of grammar, punctuation, usage, and typography—to answer specific questions that may arise during the writing process. If your paper includes tables and graphs, choose a manual that also provides guidelines on how such information should be arranged and labeled. (Both style manuals we recommend below include such guidelines and are available in many libraries and bookstores.) Early in the quarter/semester, before the almost inevitable end-of-the-term crunch, ask your instructor to recommend a manual; you can put it aside until you need it. If your instructor doesn't have a preference, we suggest *The Chicago Manual of Style*. However, since this comprehensive manual is currently available only in hardcover, at what may be a prohibitively expensive price, we also recommend the inexpensive, popular paperback edition of Kate L. Turabian's *A Manual for Writers of Term Papers, Dissertations, and Theses*, which recommends many of the same style standards suggested by *The Chicago Manual of Style*. If anxiety about standards and rules impedes your writing, don't even think about the manual until you have generated at least one draft.

A Note about Style

Some people try to compensate for uncertainty with verbal bravado: using big words and complex sentence structures to sound intelligent. Sociologists have been frequently criticized for using too much jargon and writing in a convoluted style that is difficult to comprehend. Some students try to copy that style, thinking that it will make their writing seem "academic." That defeats the purpose of writing, which is to communicate. The best writing is usually easy to read and understand. The intelligence is in the ideas not the vocabulary. Students too often think that if they sound intelligent they will get a better grade than if they write intelligently. Occasionally an instructor will give a higher grade to papers with fancy words, but most look more closely at the ideas.

So remember these tips:

- Don't use a big word where a small one will do.
- Use specialized sociological terms only to be precise about the concept you are discussing.
- Each sentence should include only one thought or idea.
- Try to use active rather than passive verbs wherever possible. That ensures that both writer and reader know *who* is "doing the doing." Too much use of the passive voice can create ambiguity about the social processes under discussion.
- Try to avoid too many prepositional phrases. Prepositional phrases can fill sentences with modifiers of modifiers and make them difficult to read.
- Use adverbs and adjectives carefully. Some people think that good writing means filling your text with flowery adverbs and adjectives. Make sure that the modifiers you use add meaning and not just filler to your text.
- Remember that reading your paper should be a pleasure, not a chore.

Chapter 4

CITATION, NOTES, AND REFERENCES

Pray be precise as to details.

SHERLOCK HOLMES IN CONAN DOYLE'S
"Adventure of the Speckled Band"

Formats for indicating the sources of quotations and borrowed ideas used in written work vary among different sociological books and journals. Your instructor may require a specific format or recommend a particular style manual. If not, the following guidelines follow one citation format widely used in sociology, illustrated in the *American Sociological Review*. In this system:

1. Author and page citations for the quotations or borrowed ideas you use are incorporated into the text of your paper.
2. Comments or additional information are included in "Notes" following the text of your paper, although such "Notes" are rarely used in undergraduate writing.
3. The full publication information for all cited materials is listed in a section at the very end, entitled either "References" or "Bibliography."

Citations in the Text

Authors' names used in the text are followed by the publication date and page number in parentheses.

Example: Matza (1969:3) states that he is presenting "a revised idea of naturalism."

The format is the same if you are paraphrasing, not quoting.

Example: Matza (1969:3) distinguishes his definition of naturalism from definitions used in the past.

When you write a textual analysis (described in Chapter 6), you might use only one source—the book or essay which you are analyzing. In this case, you need to give the publication date only the first time the author's name is mentioned.

Example (first mention of author): Durkheim (1951) claims that suicide is not only an individual event but also a social phenomenon.
(After first mention) Durkheim describes the role of social factors in suicide.

Note that the page numbers of quotations or of specific claims or evidence should be indicated even after the first mention of the author.

Example: Durkheim (44) defines suicide in a way that leaves all animal deaths out of his study.

Full publication information on the text you use for your analysis should be included in your References or Bibliography (discussed later in this chapter).
    At times you may want to cite several authors who discuss a single idea. Then you will have a series of citations which should all be enclosed within parentheses. List authors chronologically (the earliest publication date goes first) and separate the works with semicolons.

Example: Some sociologists question the value of using official statistics in conducting research (Kitsuse and Cicourel, 1963; Cicourel, 1964; Matza, 1969).

For dual authorship, give both last names; for more than two authors, use the first author's name followed by "et al." (but include all the authors' names in the References or Bibliography at the end of the paper).

Example: Many sociologists believe it is important to examine the work of the professionals who claim to treat the physical and mental health of a society (Yarrow et al., 1955; Conrad and Schneider, 1980).

For authors with more than one publication in the same year, designate each work by "a," "b," etc.

Example: Norbert Elias's *What is Sociology?*, listed below under "Examples of Listings for Books," would be cited in the text as (Elias, 1978b).

If your quotation is longer than five lines, indent all lines five spaces from the left margin (leave the right margin as it is throughout the text) and single-space. Quotation marks are unnecessary, since the indented left margin tells your reader that the material is quoted. The quotation from Durkheim, discussed in the following chapter, "Avoiding Plagiarism," is an example of a long quotation.

In rare cases, you may also use this quotation format when you want to emphasize especially important or interesting quoted material. For example, in the sample ethnographic paper in Chapter 8 the author uses the indented format to highlight quotations that are particularly dramatic but less than five lines long.

Notes

In some disciplines, footnotes (at the bottom of the page) or endnotes (following the text) contain the author and page citations which, in sociology, are incorporated into the text. In sociology, however, information which may be of interest to the reader but not directly relevant to the point of the paper may be included in a Notes section following the text. Although this practice is common among professional sociologists, it is rarely necessary in undergraduate writing. Avoid using notes as a way out of organizing your paper by making them a "dump" for materials you are not sure how to integrate. Add notes sparingly, only to express a tangential comment which you feel you *must* make.

References and Bibliographies

The Notes are followed by a list of the source materials you used in writing your paper. Some instructors prefer that you list all materials you consulted in developing your paper, whether or not they are directly incorporated into your paper; in this case the list is entitled "Bibliography." Others prefer you follow the format of most sociology journals, listing only those materials actually cited in your paper; in this case, the list is entitled "References." Check with your instructor to see which type of listing is preferred, but remember that in *both* cases, you must list the source of all borrowed ideas, whether they are directly quoted or paraphrased.

When you are compiling your Bibliography or References section, list all sources alphabetically by the author's last name. Under each author's name, list works according to the year of publication, beginning with the most recent. Do not separate the list into sections for "articles," "books," and other sources; a single list is sufficient. Do not use italics, underlining, or abbreviations, other than "ed." for "editor," "trans." for "translator," "p." for "page," or "pp." for "pages." When typing this section, center the heading, putting it all in capital letters, and triple space between the heading and the first source listed.

When the source you have cited has more than one author, both or all the authors' names should be included, in the same order in which they appear on the book's title page or after the title of the article. Alphabetize under the first author's name. The first author should be listed last name first and the other author(s) should be listed first name first. (The format is illustrated below in the examples for journal articles.)

If no author is named for a source, then list the information in alphabetical order according to title.

Example: Violations of Human Rights in Soviet-Occupied Lithuania 1978 Glenside, PA: Lithuanian American Community.

Use the examples below as models for capitalization, spacing, and punctuation of various kinds of source materials. For additional models, check the format of citations and reference entries in any issue of *American Sociological Review.* Here are some general tips.

1. Is the work a *book* whose entire main text is written by the same author or authors? If so, note that in this format titles of books are not underlined or italicized in the References or Bibliography list. If a book was first published many years ago, include the original publication date in brackets on the first line under the author's name, and the more recent date directly below it. For more than one book published in the same year by the author(s), specify each as "a," "b," and so on.

Examples of Listing for Books

Durkheim, Emile
   [1897]   Suicide. Glencoe, IL: Free Press.
   1951

Elias, Norbert
  [1939]   The Civilizing Process, Volume 2: Power and Civility, Edmund
  1982   Jephcott, trans., New York: Pantheon Books.
  1978a   The Civilizing Process, Volume 1: A History of Manners, Ed-
              mund Jephcott, trans., New York: Unizen Books.
  1978b   What is Sociology? Stephen Mennell and Grace Morrissey,
              trans., New York: Columbia University Press.
Matza, David
  1969   Becoming Deviant, Englewood Cliffs, NJ: Prentice-Hall.

2. Is the work an *article* published in a *journal?* Note that only the
first letter of the first word of the article's title is capitalized. Give the
volume number of the issue in which the article appears, and the sea-
son of publication if that is how the journal identifies its issues. Give
page numbers to help your readers locate the article.

Examples of Listings for Journal Articles

Mercy, James A. and Lala Carr Skelman
  1982   "Familial influence on the intellectual attainment in children."
              American Sociological Review 47:532–542.
Parnas, Raymond I.
  1967   "The police response to the domestic disturbance." Wisconsin
              Law Review 4 (Fall):914–960.
Yarrow, M., C. Schwartz, H. Murphy, and L. Deasy
  1955   "The psychological meaning of mental illness in the family."
              Journal of Social Issues 11:12–24.

3. Is the work found in a *collection of articles* which have been edited into an anthology? If you are referring to a specific article in the
collection, the citation goes under the name of the author of the article and includes the name of the anthology and the editor(s) within
the reference. Its capitalization and punctuation should follow the
format of a journal article, and here too you should include the page
numbers for your reader's convenience.

If you are referring to the anthology as a whole, the reference is
listed under the name of the editor(s). The format is like that of any
other book.

Examples of Listings for Collections

Conrad, Peter and Joseph W. Schneider
  1980   "Professionalization, monopoly, and the structure of medical
              practice." Pp. 155–165 in Peter Conrad and Rochelle Kern (eds.),
              The Sociology of Health and Illness, Critical Perspectives. New
              York: St. Martin's Press.

Emerson, Robert M. (ed.)
    1983   Contemporary Field Research. Boston and Toronto: Little, Brown.

4. Has the information been communicated during a *class lecture?*

Example of Listing for Lecture Notes

Lopez, David
    1989   Class lecture, October 12.

Chapter 5

AVOIDING PLAGIARISM

Careful citation is important because plagiarism is burglary—cheating which presents another writer's words or ideas as if they were your own. Plagiarism is taken very seriously in colleges and universities and can be grounds for expulsion. Instructors can usually detect intentional plagiarism. Their years of study have made them familiar with the texts and textbooks in their fields. When a student copies this writing into a paper, instructors recognize the sound and shape of the prose. Even if they can't immediately tell what page it comes from, they know it is not the student's original work. Also, plagiarized papers usually do not resemble the student's authentic writing style, which the instructor has read before, for instance, on midterm examinations.

You can avoid unintentional plagiarism by making careful notes that respect the integrity of the sources you are using, and by identifying exactly where you got borrowed words or ideas that you later use in your paper. You must cite the sources of both directly quoted words and paraphrased ideas.

Quoting a source directly means extracting a word, phrase, sentence, or passage, and inserting it, enclosed by double quotation marks or indented, according to its length, into your own paper. There are two minor changes you may make in a quotation, neither of which changes its meaning. These two legitimate changes are illustrated in our own quotation from C. Wright Mills's *The Sociological Imagination* (1959).

Every individual lives from one generation to the next, in some society; . . . he [or she] lives out a biography, and . . . he lives it out with some historical sequence. By the fact of his living he contributes, however minutely, to the shaping of his society and its history, even as he is made by society and by its historical push and shove. (6)

First, notice that we omit some of Mills's sentence, again without changing the meaning, and we indicate this omission by a punctuation mark called "ellipses," three dots. If the ellipsis points came at the end of the sentence, they would be followed by a period—hence four dots. Second, we are uneasy about Mills's use of "he" to refer to all humankind and want to make the language inclusive, so we add our own words "[or she]," inserting them within square brackets into Mills's quotation.

Another possible addition within square brackets is the Latin word *sic*, meaning "so," which you can use when you want to quote original words that contain an error. For example, in her paper at the end of Chapter 8, Sandra Ducoff Garber quotes her interview notes of a family member saying "I did the standard trick of look [*sic*] at his ear and not at his face which just drove him up the wall and he would get so frustrated and so angry."

Paraphrasing means condensing the author's meaning and translating a passage into your own words. This is a perfectly acceptable practice and, in fact, an important skill to develop. Paraphrasing forces you to think through and actively understand what you have read. But if you use another's idea when writing, you must give that person credit with a citation, even if you are presenting the idea in your own words.

There are good and bad ways to paraphrase. Here is an original passage from Emile Durkheim's *Suicide* (1951), followed by examples of good and bad paraphrasing.

The term "suicide" is applied to all cases of death resulting directly or indirectly from a positive or negative act of the victim himself, which he knows will produce this result. . . . This definition excludes from our study everything related to the suicide of animals. Our knowledge of animal intelligence does not really

Thou shalt not steal.

allow us to attribute to them an understanding anticipatory of
their death nor, especially, of the means to accomplish it. . . . If
some dogs refuse to take food on losing their masters, it is because the sadness into which they are thrown has automatically
caused lack of hunger; death has resulted, but without having
been foreseen. . . . So the special characteristics of suicide as defined by us are lacking. (44–45)

Here are two examples of bad paraphrasing. In the first, the writer
has shifted words around in the sentences and replaced individual
words by plugging in synonyms. The writer has not genuinely condensed or translated the author's meaning into her or his own words;
this problem is usually compounded by a failure to cite the source (in
this case, Durkheim):

When some pets stop eating because their owners have left, this
is caused by the unhappiness into which they have fallen, which
necessarily makes them lose their appetite: the final end that
ensues, however, was not anticipated. Therefore, the unique features of suicide as described by our definition are missing.

In the second example, the writer has changed the order but kept
the words the same. Again the writer has not condensed the passage
or translated it into her or his own words; and, again, this problem is
usually compounded by a failure to cite the source:

Lost masters cause their sad dogs, refusing food, to lack hunger.
The dogs die, not foreseeing this result. What is lacking is our
special characterization of suicide as we define it.

A good paraphrase boils down the original idea and puts it in your
own words. Here is a good paraphrase:

Example: According to Durkheim (1951:44–45), animals,
such as abandoned dogs who starve themselves, do not
commit suicide because they do not understand the connection between death and the means of causing death.

Remember that even good paraphrasing requires citing the source
of the borrowed *idea* being presented.

PART II

WRITING FROM
VARIOUS DATA SOURCES

As to Holmes, I observed that he sat frequently for half an hour on end, with knitted brows and an abstracted air, but he swept the matter away with a wave off his hand when I mentioned it. "Data! data! data!" he cried impatiently. "I can't make bricks without clay."

DR. WATSON IN CONAN DOYLE'S
"Adventure of the Copper Beeches"

The goal of a sociology paper is to develop a thesis in response to a question about the social world and to support that thesis with evidence. But where does the evidence come from?

There is no one answer. As we indicated earlier, sociology is diverse. Data may be gathered from many sources, by several methods. The next four chapters present guidelines for writing papers based on four data sources—textual analysis, library research, ethnographic field research, and quantitative research. They reflect the most typical writing assignments in sociology classes, and use or modify the formats described earlier: essay and journal (see Chapter 1). Three of the four chapters can be used from the first day of your first sociology class. Since quantitative research, however, depends on specialized ways of collecting and analyzing information, the last chapter will be more useful if you are taking or have taken a basic course in quantitative methods.

An annotated sample paper, written by an undergraduate sociology student, concludes each chapter except the one on library research.

The sample papers illustrate our guidelines. You can match them up with your own papers and use our marginal comments to check what you have written yourself.

Rather than include a sample library research paper in this section, we have instead presented information about specialized sociology reference sources because we have found that students are more likely, from their previous English classes, to be familiar with the library research paper than with the other kinds of papers assigned in sociology.

You will find the guidelines for using library references very valuable, particularly those on *Sociological Abstracts* and the *Social Science Citation Index*, since these are keys to the vast sociological literature in the library. Although our list of reference sources is not exhaustive, it will get you started in the right direction.

Papers almost always require you to do some outside reading even when data are drawn primarily from another source. For example, quantitative papers entail reviewing the literature to determine similar empirical studies of the topic, which means evaluating the books and articles which report these studies. Since this section can be helpful for proceeding in the others, we begin with how to write a textual analysis paper.

Chapter 6

THE TEXTUAL ANALYSIS PAPER

You may be assigned a paper asking you to analyze a book or portion of a book—for example, Max Weber's *The Protestant Ethic and the Spirit of Capitalism* or Erving Goffman's *The Presentation of Self in Everyday Life*. We call this method "textual" analysis because the text itself, what the author wrote, provides your data. Your paper is *about* the text itself, not about the text's subject matter. For example, a textual analysis of Durkheim's *Suicide* might concern his theory of suicide or his use of statistical data to study suicide, not suicide itself. Of course, one could write a paper about suicide based on Durkheim's book, but it would be a different kind of paper, not a textual analysis paper. Your paper is an "analysis" because you take the author's work apart to examine the different components and then put them back together. This activity is called "explication"; a textual analysis explicates, or explains, what the author's main points are and how they are connected, and offers a critique of the author's argument. An analogy would be taking a car engine apart, explaining each part and how the parts work together, and evaluating whether the car is a good buy or a lemon.

Mastering the skill of explication will help you write better papers when a textual analysis is assigned. But, perhaps as important, this skill will help you evaluate more clearly all the books and articles you encounter in your academic career.

Asking Questions about the Text

In textual analysis, the text is not only your data but also the source of your question. That is, your question will arise from the author's ideas and arguments presented in the text and your analysis of them.

51

Your question is a vehicle for conversing with the author about the thesis or argument of the work. This conversation should be conducted in an analytically critical manner, which means that to carry on your end you must raise questions about the logic of the argument, the type and credibility of the evidence, the soundness of the conclusion, and the fundamental assumptions on which the argument rests.

Your assignment may specify how you are to analyze a text, or the format may be left up to you. Here are three main areas generally addressed in a textual analysis:

1. **Summary.** What is the author saying? This is the basic question in textual analysis. It involves considering the author's main point(s). In general, most people should agree on what the author is saying. Sometimes an instructor will assign a paper asking no more than this. He or she only wants students to demonstrate that they comprehend what the author is saying. But sometimes summary is not as easy as it seems. It requires seeing the forest and not just the trees, the entire book or article, not just the particular facts that are presented to support an argument. For example, Durkheim's *Suicide* is not just about the relationship between religious denominations and suicide, but also how social structure helps explain what is commonly considered the most private of individual acts, taking one's life.

To see the whole picture of a book or article study carefully any preface, introduction, or conclusion, and the first and last chapters of a book or first and last sections of an article. Read through and think about the table of contents. What is the point of having the chapters organized the way they are? Why do the first chapters come first? Read through the section headings of the entire book or article. They usually give important clues about what the author thinks is important. They are like signposts along a highway that tell you the cities you are going through.

How does this author deal with one important sociological concept or issue in this text? Rather than analyzing all the ideas which the author presents, in this approach you focus in depth on one significant aspect of the text. If you are reading Talcott Parsons's book on the *Evolution of Societies*, for example, you might ask how Parsons views modern society. In that case, your questions would include: "How does Parsons define 'modern society'? Why, in light of the overall purpose of the book, does he discuss modern society? What evidence does he use to support his claims about it?"

2. **Analysis.** Analysis involves going beyond what the author says. It means looking at relationships: relationships between evidence and conclusions, relationships between concepts in the text, and relationships between the concepts in the work being analyzed and other texts.

What devices does the author use to convince the reader that he or she is correct? One of the general skills students should learn in college is to analyze the devices that authors—all authors, not just sociologists or academic writers—use to convince a reader. All of these have their place in writing, but all can be misused. The key here is to learn to identify what an author is doing to persuade the reader to his or her conclusions.

Logical reasoning. The most common form of logical reasoning is the syllogism (an *if/then* statement). Here the author seeks to convince you that there is a logical connection between something you already believe and something he or she wants you to believe. For example, Durkheim essentially argued that if social groups have an effect on whether a person feels a moral wholeness and if moral wholeness influences whether a person might commit suicide, then there must be a relationship between social groups and suicide. Logical reasoning can also take the form of an analogy, in which something the author wants you to understand in a certain way is compared to something you are familiar with. For example, Durkheim argues that suicide is a form of deviance, just like crime is a form of deviance. Both stem from a sense of normlessness or "anomie." There are many other logical devices that authors use, but they all have in common that the authors' arguments *make sense*. They are *logical*.

Anecdote. Anecdotes are little stories used to illustrate a point. They are especially common in journalistic accounts. A journalistic account of crime would begin with a story about a particular criminal or crime victim, with the unstated assumption that this story is representative of all criminals or victims. A single statistic can be used anecdotally to add credence to a paper. Anecdotes can make a paper "come alive" and hold the reader's interest, but do not substitute for systematic evidence.

Appeal to authority. It is quite common to show that someone the reader respects agrees with the author's perspective. This can be either an "expert" whose knowledge of a subject qualifies him or her for respect, or an elite, whose social status or position makes them believable.

Controlled study. The book or article is intended to answer a very specific empirically verifiable question such as "Are Catholics still less likely to commit suicide than Protestants?" A study designed according to the rules of the scientific method is conducted for this purpose. Durkheim rested his case on a controlled study comparing suicide rates in Protestant and Catholic areas of Europe.

Rhetorical virtuosity. This includes a number of devices that can be employed to convince a reader due to the writer's skill at using language. A well-turned phrase or metaphor that sounds poetic due to its

selection of words, e.g., baby boom, sensuous sixties, animal rights, or
law and order. Scientific jargon can give unscientific ideas the sound
of authority. Big words or convoluted sentences can make the author
sound intelligent and knowledgeable. Humor, satire, or irony can be
used to make opposing views sound ridiculous.

What is important is that the student understand what the author
is doing, to be able to analyze the devices being used.

3. **Evaluation.** How well does the author answer his or her question
and verify that answer? This is the realm of criticism (both positive
and negative). It logically comes last. You can't really judge a text
until you fully comprehend what the author is doing and how he or
she does it. It is also the most subjective stage. While an instructor
can grade how well you summarize or analyze a work, what you think
of the work is your personal opinion. There may be disagreements
about evaluation, but ultimately your opinions are your own. However, the line between analysis and evaluation is sometimes fuzzy,
and an instructor may legitimately fault you for basing your evaluation on inaccurate summary or sloppy analysis. Instructors also
have different tastes concerning how much evaluation they want.
Some want students to express their opinions about a text, others just
want summary and/or analysis. Evaluation involves asking the following questions:

Is the argument of the text clear? Is it clear what question the text
is attempting to answer? Are the definitions precise and unambiguous? Are the concepts appropriate to the questions addressed? Are the
conclusions explicitly presented or scattered throughout? This dimen-
sion of evaluation concerns the summary. If the summary is easy to
do, the text rates highly on this criterion.

Does the author make valid assumptions? Identifying and evaluating an author's assumptions are two of the intellectual skills often de-
manded in sociological theory classes. Authors necessarily make
assumptions about the way the world works. For example, some theories assume that human beings act primarily on the basis of material self-interest, others assume that they are motivated by the need
for social approval. Some theories treat society as the aggregation of
individuals, assuming that all social behavior should be reduced to
individual behavior. Others assume that there are factors such as social class that can only be understood at the given level of society.
Evaluating such assumptions means identifying the author's assumptions to see how plausible they are.

**How well does the text use evidence? Is the evidence adequate to
the conclusions?** If the text is based on a specific study, how well is it
performed? If the evidence is less systematic, does it seem to be fairly
drawn or carefully selected to favor the author's point of view? This is

an area where many beginning students feel ill equipped because they have not been thoroughly trained in methods and may feel they don't know enough about a topic to gauge whether or not the evidence is selective. Some instructors, while admitting such limitations, encourage students to make a stab at this type of evaluation. Most students should have some sense of whether the evidence presented adequately supports the conclusion. One can ask, "Even if this evidence is true, does the author's conclusion necessarily follow?" You will find that the answer is often no.

Are the conclusions and implications supported by other works? There are times when we assume that other works have validity and therefore we compare the text being studied to other works. This is especially common where certain works have achieved a sort of "orthodoxy," at least by some sociologists. One might ask, for example, whether a work by a contemporary writer on deviance legitimately qualifies as a Durkheimian analysis.

Is the craftsmanship of the writing sound? Do the parts fit into a whole? Is the prose understandable? Do the ideas smoothly flow from one to another? Craftsmanship is basically the theme of this book. If you were grading the text according to the criteria we have set forth as good writing, how would that text stand up?

It is important to repeat that different instructors have different tastes concerning how much evaluation they want and along what criteria. Some want you to basically stick to the text itself. Others want the text evaluated relative to other works. Some emphasize an evaluation of the logic, others of the evidence, others of the assumptions, etc. Make sure you understand what the instructor's preferences are.

Compare-and-Contrast Assignments

If you are asked to compare and/or contrast two authors' works (or two works by the same author), you must start by identifying the common topic under consideration and use that as the basis for your question. How do these two works deal with an issue which is central to each?

Any or all of these three aspects (summary, analysis, evaluation) may be relevant to the particular work you are considering. Before you decide which questions will form the basis of your paper, you must read the text—and you must read it in a special way. We recommend that you buy your own copy of the book you will be using, if it is affordable. You will then be able to mark it up.

How to Read the Text

Before developing your question, get to know the text. As you read, keep in mind three general tasks. First, you must *identify the main points* that are explicitly presented as parts of the argument. Second, you must *identify the author's hidden assumptions*—that is, what she or he takes for granted about how the world works, and does not question or bother to justify. These assumptions are like the principles of physics taken for granted in building an engine. Third, you must *evaluate* the text, asking, for example, in what ways the argument is not convincing. What are its problems? How could it be better? Evaluating the argument is like diagnosing which of a car's engine parts do not work and how they could work, or arguing that the whole thing should be junked and stating why.

In other words, as you read you must ask yourself and ask the text the same sorts of questions that you will address in your paper. Here is a more detailed description of the close reading required for textual analysis:

Getting to Know Something about the Text

Here are some things you must find out in order to become acquainted with the text:

Who is the author? What is her or his background? This information is sometimes included in the introduction of the book. If there is no biographical information in the introduction, or if the information is insufficient to give you a picture of the author, there are resources you can use to find out the information.

The *Biography and Genealogy Master Index* contains a list of authors' names, followed by a list of references in which you will find biographical information. The reference book titles are abbreviated; consult the front of the book for the complete titles.

Information on well-known authors—for example, the founders of the discipline—might also be found in *Encyclopaedia Britannica, Encyclopedia Americana,* or the *International Encyclopedia of the Social Sciences.*

When was the text written? What was the social climate of the period? To determine when the text was written look at the copyright date in the front of the book. If you find more than one date, the first one indicates the date of the original printing or first edition. To determine the historical period in which the text was written look first to your introduction. If this does not provide adequate information, you can use the sources above, paying particular attention to the historical information given in entries on the author or the countries where the author lived.

What is the polemical context—that is, where is the text located in the ongoing debate on the question? To whom is the author responding? Sometimes the text will reveal the polemical context by explicitly contrasting the author's argument with other perspectives. This information may be found either in the body of the text or in the preface or introduction. Sometimes it requires reading between the lines, paying attention to how the author refers to other works, for example, by drawing contrasts between her or his position and that of others. If the polemical context is not obvious, look for other books or journal articles about the author or the subject of the text. Often scholars write critiques or commentaries on others' work, especially if it is considered controversial or exemplary. This literature can be found in the library. (See Chapter 7 for guidelines about specific references.) Remember, the reference librarian can help you locate sources to help you get the information you need to write your paper.

Reading Twice

Read the text twice, for different purposes.

First, read for the big picture—get a feel for the text's organization and content. The author has major points that you are looking for. These major points, in turn, are supported by minor points. Pay special attention to the author's introduction, often called a preface, or to a foreword, written by an expert in the field.

After you have completed this preliminary reading, focus on the kind of question you will be addressing in your paper. If your instructor has specified a question, now is the time to consider it carefully and be sure you understand what information to provide, how deeply to analyze the work, and how much of your own opinion to give. If the assignment is more general, look back over the categories of questions we listed above and decide which approach you will take: Will you analyze the text as a whole? Would you rather focus on a particular concept or aspect of the argument? Or should you compare this work to another one?

With your question in mind, read the text very closely the second time through; this reading forms the core of your "data collection." Your goal is to understand the interconnected points that constitute the author's argument and to record these important points on note cards. Note-taking during this second reading is an important step toward writing your paper. We will deal with it in detail below.

What are you looking for in this detailed reading? Look for the author's argument—that is, the question that the author is trying to answer and the evidence she or he used to answer it. The following questions will assist you in identifying the text's argument, that is, the author's main points and the assumptions hidden beneath them:

- What is the author's question? For example, in *Suicide*, Durkeim asks, "What are the social factors that help explain suicide?"
- What is the author's answer—that is, what provides the core of the argument? What answers have other scholars given? Durkheim argues that the degree of social solidarity within groups that people belong to affects how likely they are to commit suicide. Protestants were more likely to commit suicide (when Durkheim lived) because Catholicism provided greater social solidarity. He was trying to demonstrate that psychological explanations that emphasized individual pathology were not sufficient.
- What evidence does the author offer to support this answer? Is the evidence logical or empirical or both? Does the evidence actually support the argument?
- How does the author get from point A to point B? How do the main points that you identified in your reading relate to one another?
- What are the assumptions? What does the author take for granted, points without which the argument could not be made? Some examples of fundamental assumptions are that people have free will, that our social order constitutes the normal state of affairs, or that free enterprise benefits everyone.

As you engage in this second reading, you may want to adjust your question. If you planned on analyzing the text as a whole, for example, you may now discover that for this particular paper that task is too broad. If you attempt to explicate a work that is too comprehensive, your analysis may touch on a little bit of everything but fail to cover anything in depth; the result will be a weak analysis. Conversely, you may discover that it is not possible to discuss one concept without analyzing the text as a whole, or to explain this text without comparing or contrasting it with another work. If your focus is *too* narrow, your analysis won't make sense. In any case, remember as you read to adjust the breadth of your questioning to the particular materials you wish to analyze.

Taking Notes

In textual analysis, you will find note-taking a valuable tool for gaining access to the author's argument. Taking notes is a personal skill which varies somewhat from student to student. You might take very detailed notes on separate note cards or simply outline the main points. Whichever method you use, check its effectiveness. For example, after you have read your text for the second time, ask yourself the questions listed above under "Reading Twice." If you cannot answer them, you may need to read the text more closely or change your note-taking technique.

In general, you should paraphrase the original text when taking notes. This means you should boil it down and put it in your own words. (See Chapter 7 for tips on effective note-taking.) You should quote only in a few special instances:

1. When the original is worded so elegantly, memorably, or powerfully that you do not want to change its effect.
2. When you just can't paraphrase it and do justice to the meaning, even though you have tried.
3. When the original is provocative or unusual, and you want to borrow the prestige of the original author to run defense for yourself, in case your reader disagrees with this point. Our own epigraphs illustrate the power of a distinguished author's exact words to enhance an argument.
4. When you want to do an extensive analysis on one small passage (an exegesis).

When you want to use the author's exact words, be sure to mark them as a quotation on your note card so that you will properly cite the source in your paper. You must also document paraphrases (see Chapter 5).

Organizing Your Paper

Once you have read the text carefully and made notes on the most revealing passages, then you must outline your analysis and plan how to present it. The essay format is more suitable than journal format for textual analysis (see "Developing an Argument: Logic and Structure" in Chapter 1). Within the basic format there are a number of ways in which you can organize your paper. Here are three basic outline patterns you can use or modify:

I. *Organize the body of your paper into three main parts corresponding to the three main tasks involved in explication:*
   1. Summary: Your description of what the author is saying, the author's main points.
   2. Analysis: Your explanation of what is behind the author's argument, for example, the polemical context or debate being addressed, the author's hidden assumptions, the author's evidence, implications of the author's points, etc.

3. Evaluation: Your assessment of the strengths and weaknesses of the author's argument. How well do the main points fit together? How relevant is the evidence to the points being made? How convincing are the conclusions?

II. *Organize the body of your paper into major points which assert what you believe is most important about the text:*
1. In your introduction, identify the most important features and state your position. You might also want to state the positions of other scholars unless your assignment excludes the use of outside sources.
2. In the second paragraph (or section, in a longer paper), summarize one main point you want the reader to know in order to accept your point of view and provide detailed evidence from the text to support this point.
3. Do the same thing in the third and fourth paragraphs (or sections), presenting one more major point in each.
4. In your conclusion restate your claims and summarize your points supporting them.

III. *Organize your paper around comparing and contrasting:*

There are two basic patterns you can follow to compare and contrast two works:

Pattern I	Pattern II
A (1st author)	1 (1st Point)
1 (1st point)	A (1st author)
2 (2nd point)	B (2nd author)
3 (3rd point)	2 (2nd point)
B (2nd author)	A (1st author)
1 (1st point)	B (2nd author)
2 (2nd point)	3 (3rd point)
3 (3rd point)	A (1st author)
	B (2nd author)

Writing Your Textual Analysis

Generally, your goal is to answer in writing, in a logical and coherent way, the same questions you have been asking about the text as you read. A review of "Developing an Argument: Logic and Structure" in Chapter 1 will help you in this task. A tip for developing a cohesive paper is to refer back to the questions you are answering as you write. They can serve as a guide in determining which information you need to make your point, and which is extraneous. Keeping your key questions in mind as you write and revise will keep you from wandering. Remember to identify the author and text in your opening paragraph. When writing a research paper, you must follow a special set of formal conventions for documentation. For textual analysis, however, it is usually sufficient to indicate only in the first reference the publication date of the text you are using. Thereafter you may document quotations with the author's name and appropriate page number. When referring to an idea or argument found more generally throughout the text, the author's name alone, included in one of your own sentences (for example, "Elias states . . ."), will suffice. See page 65 for illustrations of these special citation formats. Consult your instructor for clarification and for her or his preference.

A Sample Student Paper

Lysa Agundez's paper was written for a course in "Culture and Personality." The text she chose to analyze is Norbert Elias's *The Civilizing Process*. It was an appropriate choice because Elias's goal is to show how individual psyches and actions take the same shape as the social structure in which they occur. We selected Lysa's paper not only because it illustrates a concise summary of a complex sociological work, but because of its gritty and interesting subject. Here Lysa attempts to show how Elias uses the sociological imagination to connect the most personal of experiences with large-scale social relations.

Lysa identified and designed her paper around two key issues in the text she analyzed. The format of her paper is, accordingly, a variation of the "Three-Part Essay" format—in this case, a "Two-Part" format. Our comments on the pages facing the paper will indicate how she addressed the three questions we have recommended you consider in any textual analysis: What is the author saying (summary)? What devices does the author use to convince the reader that he or she is correct (analysis)? How well does the author answer his or her question and verify the answer (evaluation)?

Demonstrating a problem many students encounter, Lysa's summary is more complete than her analysis and evaluation. Follow both her well-written paper and our remarks to see the strengths of her work, and how it could be made even better.

OUR COMMENTS

Because of the length of her paper, Lysa included a title page, as suggested in Chapter 11.

Norbert Elias on the Development of Civilization
through Repression of Instincts

Lysa Agundez
Sociology 134
Professor Heritage
March 23, 1990

"The nature of this essay" is a vague phrase, and its meaning is unclear. It would be more effective to say: "This essay will address the two most important aspects of Elias's work," or "I will address two important issues raised by Elias."

Note that Lysa plans to address only two issues. Nowhere is it carved in stone that the student *must* have three main points (unless, of course, the assignment specifically says so). Since Lysa has identified two truly key ideas, her paper will have enough substance.

The second paragraph begins Lysa's summary of the first point she intends to address. Her summary is longer and more complete than the analysis and evaluation sections which follow. Although this is a drawback to her paper, in the case of writing as complex as that of Elias, we give her credit just for being able to identify and describe his main points.

Lysa's paper should include a bibliography or reference page, including the publication information on both volumes. As you will see, this is a serious shortcoming of her paper.

While it is helpful to make it clear which ideas expressed are being attributed to Elias, it is a good idea to vary the form of attribution. The repetition of, "Elias believes," in this paragraph could have been avoided by using, "Elias argues," "Elias maintains," "Elias contends," or other phrases.

This paper will discuss the theories of Norbert Elias, who argues that the development of civilization involves a repression of instincts. The nature of this essay entails addressing two issues: (1) The stricter control of emotion and behavior developed following the Middle Ages; and (2) The relationship of shame and the structure of society. Then I will discuss Elias's distinctive contributions to investigation of the civilizing process.

Norbert Elias is a German sociologist, whose two-volume masterpiece is titled The Civilizing Process. The first volume, titled The History of Manners, is a complete presentation of basic attitude changes of European manners and morals. Examples include attitudes towards bodily functions, table manners, sexual behavior, and aggression. The second volume, titled Power and Civility, presents a thorough sociological analysis of the development of civilized behavior formed by the centralization of society.

The process of civilization, Elias believes, involved a progressively stricter control of emotion and habits of restraint which led to socially institutionalized frontiers of shame and emotional standards. Thus, the growth of civilization, Elias believes, involves the gradual intensification of instinctual repression over the centuries. In The History of Manners, Elias documents the gradual domestication of human affects and emotions from the Middle Ages to our days. His purpose is to show how the psychical make-up of modern men and women differs in significant ways from their ancestors. Compared to modern man, medieval people, Elias argues, were faced with few barriers to the acting out of affect, be that in the area of aggression, sex, at the dinner table, or in the bedroom.

To prove his point, Elias turns to various etiquette and manners books that have been steadily written and very widely read since the days of Erasmus of Rotterdam. Written mainly for members of European court society, these books exemplify right and wrong behavior. Systematically comparing their changing content over time, Elias takes them as guides to the changing life-styles and sense of propriety on the passing historical scene.

Lysa's use of these examples as evidence for her explication would be strengthened by citing their sources in Elias's text. In fact, with material as colorful as this, direct quotation would liven up the scholarly discussion and keep the reader's interest.

The quotation marks around "natural" are not necessary, since the word is not being quoted or used ironically or in a special way.

Lysa does a good job of summarizing the advice offered in the etiquette books which serve as Elias's data. More direct quotations would provide the reader with a stronger sense of the materials he used to reach his conclusions.

It is acceptable to use language normally considered vulgar to describe a historical situation, especially if it is used in the text. Still, if it makes you uncomfortable, or you think it might offend your instructor, you can adopt a euphemism.

Many of the teachings of Erasmus's book of manners would
be taken for granted by most children today. For example,
medieval writers tell their readers in quest for refinements
of manners that one should not gnaw a bone and then throw it
back into the common dish, that diners should not wipe their
nose on their hands or spit into the plate, nor poke in their
mouth, nor scratch themselves while eating. These elementary
rules were necessary for fifteenth century feudal nobles,
who, in fact, ate with their hands, threw bones to dogs
gathered around the table, dipped their fingers in common
dishes, and drank from a common goblet.

By the sixteenth century, however, the time of Erasmus,
standards became gradually more demanding, and people more
self-conscious of their public manners. As time went on,
eating habits gradually became more refined. People began to
use forks instead of searching with pieces of bread for
chunks of meat in the common pot. They were taught that they
should use their knives unobtrusively so as not to threaten
their neighbors at the table.

Erasmus, in an effort to teach "civility" to the
nobility and the aspiring bourgeoisie, did not limit his
advice to table manners. With a lack of embarrassment that
might seem gross to modern sensibilities, he attempted to
teach his public the circumstances in which spitting,
farting, urinating, or defecating in public might or might
not be defensible.

Spitting, for instance, was a common "natural" bodily
function in the Middle Ages. As a matter of fact, it was even
considered a custom and was commonplace in the courts of
feudal lords. The only major restriction imposed then was
that "one should not spit on or over the table but under it"
(I:156). In the sixteenth century, people were provided with
spittoons. And in our age, the "need" for spitting in public
has been altogether abolished.

Farting in public also became prohibited over the
civilizing process. In the Middle Ages, it was considered
unhealthy to "hold back wind" (I:130). It was better to be
emitted with a noise than to be held back. Gradually,
however, the feeling of embarrassment increased, and it was
instructed to calm your body by farting only while covering

"Polite etiquette guides" is redundant, since etiquette by definition involves politeness. Never use two words when one will do!

The contrast between the reader's stereotypical image of Versailles as a glamorous place and the graphic insight Lysa provides about the use of perfume stimulates a lot of reader interest.

In using "complementary movements," Lysa seems to be making a valiant effort to avoid repetitive use of "changes." Still, since (particularly in sociology) "movement" implies a collective effort of some sort, it is somewhat confusing here.

In general, Lysa makes good use of the kinds of transition words discussed in Chapter 10. In this case, "moreover" indicates to the reader that what she reports in this paragraph is additional information relevant to what was discussed in the one preceding.

Did you catch "conceled" as a misspelling of "concealed"? Always proof your final draft for spelling errors, which detract from your presentation and make your ideas more difficult to follow. If you are using a word processor, a spelling check can be done electronically. See Chapter 11 for tips on correcting misspellings in your final draft.

Since "threshold of shame" is a special term which conveys one of Elias's key concepts, it would be good to define or explain it here, to be sure the reader knows what it means and how it is being used.

the sounds with coughs, or, if one was in a holy place, to press your buttocks together. By the eighteenth century, farting, like spitting, was abolished.

People furthermore used to urinate and defecate in public, and polite etiquette guides simply taught their readers that one should avoid looking at people engaging in these activities. Even in the Palace of Versailles, people used to relieve themselves in corridors and on staircases. As a result, a huge consumption of perfume at the court was required to hide the offensive odors in the palace.

To Elias, these changes are not just curious: they indicate basic changes in the ways human beings perceive themselves and use their bodies in relation to those of others. People now began to mold themselves and others more self-consciously and deliberately than was the wont and use of the Middle Ages. Much of what we now consider "second nature" was the result of a century-long process of gradual domestication. As external restraint against personal emissions gave way to self-restraint, an "invisible wall" gradually grew up between one human body and another.

Elias also documents complementary movements involving sleeping habits and sexuality. Here, also, the public became distinguished from the private sphere. In medieval society it was quite normal for many people, even strangers, to spend the night in one room and even to share the same bed. Today, however, the bedroom has become privatized and separated from the rest of social life.

Moreover, in the Middle Ages it was customary for guests at a wedding to terminate the proceedings by undressing the bride and groom who were then obliged to consummate the marriage in the presence of the assembled company. By the late Middle Ages, the custom gradually changed to the extent that the couple was placed on the bed fully dressed. After this period, sexual life was conceled and dismissed behind the scenes altogether.

Elias argues that these examples of changes in sexual behavior, along with those illustrating changes in standards of self-restraint, mark the advance in the threshold of shame. Noting that restrictions of various kinds surround the elimination of natural functions in many societies, both

Note that, in contrast to the use of quotation marks around "natural" on page 67, their use with "primitive" and "civilized" are appropriate here, since Lysa is using the words to indicate certain analytic definitions of those terms.

This is where Lysa begins her summary of the second point she introduced in the opening paragraph. It is not covered as fully as the first one was.

Because of this quotation's length, Lysa has appropriately indented and single-spaced it.

Here is a good example of why it is important to include full publication information for references: When we went to look for more information on this quotation (in this case, to check on correct punctuation), we could not find it on page 8 of our copy of the second volume. Perhaps it is because Lysa used a different edition than we have, but, since no publication information is provided, we cannot tell for sure.

When Lysa claims that Elias's thesis is "convincing," it sounds like she is ready to begin an evaluation of the text. However, she continues her summary without giving the reader any evidence of *why* she believes the thesis is convincing. See the following page for tips on how she might evaluate the text.

"primitive" and "civilized," he concludes that the fears of
natural elimination and the feeling of shame and repugnance
in which it is expressed does not originate from a rational
understanding of the origins of certain diseases, as one
might think. Actually, our understanding of their dangers is
attained only in the nineteenth century, at a very late stage
in the civilizing process.

Elias argues that our feelings of distaste and shame are
based on changes in the ways people live together in the
structure of society. He discusses these changes in social
structure at length in Power and Civility, in which he
announces:

> . . . [T]he civilizing of conduct and the corresponding
> transformation of human consciousness and libidinal
> make-up cannot be understood without tracing the process
> of state formation, and within it the advancing
> centralization of society which first finds particularly
> visible expression in the absolute form of life (II:8).

Despite the cumbersome formulation, Elias's basic thesis
is unexpectedly simple and convincing: as society became more
centralized, individuals came into close contact and began to
exercise greater self-constraint—"more affect control," in
Elias's jargon.

For example, Elias believes feudal knights behaved like
powerful and uninhibited children. These knights vigorously
(and often violently) engaged in self-defense and
self-gratification, clearly demonstrating minimal manners.
"What was lacking," Elias observes of this impulsive
personality, "was the invisible wall of affects which seems
now to rise between one body and another, repelling and
separating"(II:256). The courtiers who congregated later in
absolutist courts were far more careful types; relying now on
central royal authority for physical protection, they vied
(rarely violently) for influence and advancement.
Consequently, the feudal knights increasingly had to regulate
their behavior to secure protection and promotions.

Again, Lysa has used quotation marks correctly here, since "courtoisie" is a foreign word. (By the way, it might have been interesting if she had pointed out how it demonstrates the way the tips Erasmus provided became the basis for our idea of (and word for) "courtesy.")

But why does the phrase "invisible walls" also have quotation marks around it? If it is directly from Elias's work, there should be a citation for it.

By including the concept of "sociological imagination," Lysa is demonstrating her familiarity with basic sociological principles. However, she could apply the idea more fully here. "Sociological imagination" does not just mean using an imaginative approach to research. It involves relating individual experience to large-scale social structures and processes; Elias does this very well by connecting personal habits to the historical formation of a centralized political state.

To strengthen her paper, at this point Lysa could have begun an analysis of Elias's work, making clear the ways in which Elias goes about convincing the reader to accept his point of view. (He uses empirical data written during the time he's theorizing about.)

Lysa's evaluation of the text should follow her analysis. This is where she might tell the reader why she believes Elias's basic thesis is "convincing" (perhaps because the data are contemporaneous with social changes that are taking place in people's everyday lives.) Alternatively, she might choose to criticize how Elias attempts to justify his argument. (She could, for example, question whether etiquette books, however "juicy" and graphic, are accurate representations of how people live: would you consider "Dear Abby" books one author's perspective on relations among those in a certain social class reflective of *your* everyday life?)

Sometimes students neglect to include criticisms of work they are analyzing because they are afraid it will undermine the strengths pointed out in their papers. However, including Thomas's critique adds to Lysa's paper by showing she is aware of the intellectual discussion he has generated. Unfortunately, there is no citation for Thomas, so there is no way for the reader to judge his credibility or to further investigate his assessment of Elias.

Rather than expressing the author's personal feelings, the conclusion should bring the reader full circle by summarizing or drawing conclusions about the work being discussed or its significance.

Furthermore, crude feudal "courtoisie" was replaced by a more exacting code as courtiers strived to maintain their status, fending off the bourgeoisie below. The threshold of shame and embarrassment rose and rational forethought became a more important guide to conduct; bodily functions hidden, spontaneous impulses suppressed, and more elaborate proprieties established. Henceforth those "invisible walls" were everywhere, creating private selves who anxiously calculated their actions, thereby increasing self-control over passions and emotions.

Elias's ideas are similar to those of other authors, such as Sigmund Freud. So what makes for the distinctive contribution of this book? It is Elias's true leap of the sociological imagination when searching for data through which this process might be documented; his use of etiquette manuals was very creative, and his research was very thorough. Even though his work was published forty years after it was written, it is not at all outdated. In fact, it is encompassing and stands complete today.

One might argue that Elias's focus is too narrow. Elias chose to focus only on the transformation of people from the Middle Ages to our times and has eschewed the occasion for a comparative treatment of the subject. As Keith Thomas (1978) has pointed out, Elias says next to nothing about the world of Graeco-Roman antiquity in which a similar process had surely taken place, even though the results of that process were largely lost during the Dark Ages. There is next to nothing in the book about other high civilizations, such as those of Asia, in which one can discern similar trends. But these are, after all, minor matters. One can hardly reproach an author who has given so much for not having written a world history of manners.

In conclusion, I was very happy that I got to work on such an interesting topic. I think one can learn from Elias's detailed method of research—looking in countless manners books and presenting the material the way things really happened and then giving a thorough sociological explanation of civilization.

Chapter 7

THE LIBRARY
RESEARCH PAPER

A library research paper requires you to use the library in two ways: first, to develop the question that you will address in your paper if it hasn't been assigned; and, second, to collect the information that you will use to support your paper's thesis. In order to prepare your paper, you must know how to ask a good sociological question (see Chapter 1) and how to use the library effectively. Most library research papers require the following steps.

Scheduling Your Time

Work backward with your time grid (see Chapter 2), making deadlines for stages in your project, such as choosing a topic, beginning research, recording information, organizing an outline, drafting the paper, revising it, and writing the final version.

Scheduling your time is important with a library research paper because if your library doesn't have crucial books and articles, you will have to order them through a service (often free) called interlibrary loan. Interlibrary loan is a way to borrow books temporarily from other libraries. Your own college librarian can usually arrange for this service if you need to read material which is not in your library. But the interlibrary loan service takes time. Therefore, you must start working on the project as soon as possible to allow time for all the steps and, if necessary, to allow time to order and receive material.

Before You Go to the Library: Choosing a Topic

You often start a library research project not knowing much about your topic. How, then, do you begin to develop a good question?

First, you must select a general subject area—an area that is relevant to the concerns of your course and of interest to you. One way to find a topic is to skim your syllabus and course readings. Be sure to consider the entire syllabus, since a topic that will be discussed later in the course might be the basis for a good research question. Your instructor can help at this stage by letting you know if your topic is too broad or too far afield.

Next, even before going to the library, construct some provisional questions. For example, let's say you want to study the feminist movement in the United States. Ask yourself why this topic interests you. Your personal interest in a subject not only motivates you during the research and writing process; it can also guide you to ask a good question. Also ask yourself what specific aspect of the subject you want to investigate for this particular class assignment, and what specifically you want to know about it. In the case of feminism, for example, you may want to focus your research on differences in wages (such as, "Are women's wages lower than men's?"), on power differences (such as, "Why do unequal power relations exist between men and women?"), or on ways people learn to fill the gender roles expected of them (such as, "How are males and females socialized to enact sex role stereotypes in their daily lives?").

Remember to maintain a sociological perspective on the subject. The examples given in the previous paragraph, for instance, are sociologically relevant because they are concerned with differences between groups of people (men and women) and because they focus on patterned relationships in the social world. A review of Chapter 1 will help stimulate the sociological imagination you need to ask a good question.

Once you have narrowed your topic and begun to shape it into a question, it's time to go to the library.

Using the Library to Review the Sociological Literature

Begin your work in the library by getting an overview of the sociological research which has already been conducted into your question. (The "Locating References" section that follows will help you in this.) This overview of research published in books and journal articles is called "a review of the literature." ("Literature" in this sense, of course, has nothing to do with fiction and poetry.) "Reviewing the literature" in sociology involves discovering whether scholarly research has been published on the question you tentatively have in mind, how the question was formulated, and what answers have been suggested.

Reviewing the literature will help you in two important and inter-
related ways. First, a review of the literature helps you to refine your
question. How has the question been framed before? Has more than
one plausible answer been suggested as a result of empirical or theoretical research? Remember as you fine-tune your question that you
must be able to find sufficient evidence to support the answer you
will propose, and that it must be specific enough to be researchable
within the time frame of your assignment. Second, reviewing the literature helps you to identify those books and journal articles which
contain reports of research into the question you are addressing in
your paper. The quality of your paper will depend on how thoroughly
you locate such research; it is the "data" you will use to support your
thesis. Once you locate relevant books and articles, you will take in-
depth notes on them.

Locating Specialized Sociological References

The key to the library is the reference section. The reference librarians are there to answer your questions and help you find the appropriate books, articles, journals, and abstracts for your project.

If your course textbooks include sections on "Recommended Reading," often located at the ends of chapters, you can start with those
references, choosing suggested books and articles that seem most appropriate. Start with the most recently published sources because
they include references to earlier works.

Be aware that, unlike most papers for high school, for a college research paper you will be expected to consult articles in specialized
professional journals. In the last section of this chapter you will find
an annotated list of journals commonly used by sociologists.

In addition to any references you find in your texts, you should begin your research with the following five library resources on which
sociology students rely:

- *Catalog*
- *Sociological Abstracts*
- *Social Science Citation Index*
- *Social Science Index*
- *International Encyclopedia of the Social Sciences*

Catalog

Use the catalog to find suitable books in your library. Library books
may be identified on index cards in drawers. Or books my be listed on
celluloid microfiches which you must read in special machines to
magnify this information. Or your library may catalog its books with

a computerized system which displays this information on a screen; and with some computerized online systems you can print out your own copy of appropriate information. In all three cases, only the equipment changes; the books are organized in the same way—according to author's name, title, and subject.

Finding information by looking in the catalog under author and title is relatively straightforward. But if you look under a subject for books about your topic and don't find any information, it may be because the subject you are looking under is not an official subject category. For example, if you look in the catalog under "Coping," you will not find anything. "Coping" is not an official topic. In this case, you must consult a special reference book to find official topics (called "subject headings"). This special reference book is a large red two-volume set called *The Library of Congress Subject Headings* and is usually placed near the catalog. For example, if you look up "Coping" in *The Library of Congress Subject Headings*, you will find these instructions:

Coping. *See* Adjustment (Psychology).

That means that you should look under "Adjustment (Psychology)" in the catalog to find books on coping. As another example, if you want to find books on fraternities, *The Library of Congress Subject Headings* tells you to look in the catalog under the official topic "Greek letter societies."

Sociological Abstracts

This reference is published as a set of volumes each year. *Sociological Abstracts* gives more than bibliographic information. It also provides abstracts of articles published in major sociological journals. (An abstract is a summary of an article.) Learning to use *Sociological Abstracts* will save you much time, since these summaries will allow you to decide whether the sources themselves are relevant to your topic. In this way you can weed some out without having to locate and read them.

To use *Sociological Abstracts*, follow these two steps:

Step One—Locate the index volume for a recent year. Here you will find subject headings. Under the headings will be references to abstracts. Each abstract has its own unique number. For example, under the subject heading of "Mental illness/Mentally ill" you will find the information shown in Figure 7-1. Jot down the number at the end of any references to abstracts that look potentially useful, for example, N7474. These numbers are not page numbers. They are abstract numbers. Each abstract, in another volume, has its own number, like N7474.

Figure 7-1   Index Entry from *Sociological Abstracts*

Mental illness/Mentally ill
accommodation processes, informal treatment of mental illness; case study
data collected by students; troublesome individuals not receiving formal
treatment; N7474
health breakdown, mental/phyical illness susceptibility; social support
insufficiency/disruption; N7412
inferences of mental illness; social noninvolvement; experiment, videotapes;
college students; N7392
medical/sociological characteristics of pronoia/paranoia; comments, reply;
N7459

Step Two—Now look up the abstract by its number in a separate
volume which is usually shelved next to the index volume. This abstract will give a summary of the article and bibliographic information telling you where the complete article can be found. Papers delivered at conferences are also summarized in the abstracts. When using the abstracts, make sure you are aware of the sources of articles, since it may be very difficult for you to find papers that are delivered at conferences and have not been published. For example, if your topic is on accommodation processes, then you would look up the number N7474 and find the abstract shown in Figure 7-2. The

Figure 7-2   Text Entry from *Sociological Abstracts*

84 = 1984
N 7474 = abstract number

84N7474

Lynch, Michael (School Social Sciences U California, Irvine 92717),
Accommodation Practices: Vernacular Treatments of Madness, UM
Social Problems, 1983, 31, 2, Dec, 152-164.

¶ Commitment to mental hospitals normally follows a period of informal attempts at accommodation by family & friends. The nature of these accommodation processes is examined on the basis of data collected for term papers by students in classes on the sociology of mental illness; each paper described a person who, though not classified as mentally ill, was a persistent source of trouble for others, & also described the accommodation processes used in coping with the troublesome behavior. Three classes of accommodation practices are identified: minimizing contact by avoiding or ignoring the troublemaker; managing the troublemaker's actions by humoring, screening, taking over, orienting to a varying level of normality, & practical jokes & retaliations; & influencing reactions to the troublemaker, including producing notoriety, shadowing, giving advance warning, hiding & diluting the troublemaker, & covering up. These processes reveal the role of groups & organizations in constructing normality. 24 References. Modified HA bibliographic information indicates that this article was published in the journal *Social Problems,* which is found in most libraries. If you already have an author's name and want an abstract of the article, you can start looking in the index volume under authors' names, not subject headings (see Figure 7-3). Locating N7474 is the same as step two above.

It is helpful to go through these indexes by annual volume in order to become familiar with new published sources for your research. At the end of each year, a cumulative index is compiled that you can refer to and save time by not having to search through each individual volume.

Social Science Citation Index

This annual multivolume work, like *Sociological Abstracts,* provides bibliographic information. But the *Social Science Citation Index* gives other information and is a unique and invaluable reference source for undergraduates and established scholars alike. Its main special feature is the way it identifies the references that authors cite in their own articles (hence the word "citation" in its title). This feature allows you to trace the interconnected network of a research tradition and see which scholars' work influenced which other scholars. Two other features of the work enable you to find information through key words in titles and by authors' academic or corporate affiliation. Because so much information, often abbreviated, is compressed into this source, and the print is quite small, do not expect to find the *Social Science Citation Index* easy to decipher and read. However, with some examples, like the ones to follow to guide you in understanding its organization, and with some brief experience using it, you will find the *Social Science Citation Index* an indispensable reference tool.

Each annual set of the complete *Social Science Citation Index* includes these four volumes:

- *Source Index*
- *Citation Index*
- *Subject Index*
- *Corporate Index*

Figure 7-3 Index Entry from *Sociological Abstracts*

Lyman, Stanford M., N7208, N7240
Lynch, Michael, N7474
Lynn, Richard, N8361

To use the *Social Science Citation Index* follow these corresponding four steps:

Step One—Look in a recent year's *Source Index* to find bibliographic information about current work by a particular author, for example, Michael Lynch, a scholar cited in the sample ethnographic field research paper in Chapter 8. Figure 7-4, an entry from the 1984 *Source Index*, provides information on the current work of anyone identified as M. Lynch, including this Michael Lynch. The information is abbreviated and often requires some detective work to decipher and confirm by cross-checking. From this list you can tell that in his article "Accommodation Practices: Vernacular Treatments of Madness," M. Lynch (who's really Michael Lynch) cites 24 other sources, including, for example, an article by E. M. Lemert, published in 1962 in a journal entitled *Sociometry*, volume 25, beginning on page 2.

Step Two—Look in that year's *Citation Index* to find articles that cite earlier known works by a particular author. Use this volume to go from other publications to the more recent, related articles that cite them (see Figure 7-5). By cross-checking this information with *Sociological Abstracts* and with the *Source Index* in *Social Science Citation Index*, you can establish that one of these references is to the Michael Lynch who wrote "Accommodation Practices: Vernacular Treatments of Madness," but that the other references are to other authors named "M. Lynch." For example, the reference in bold type to "83 AM WAY MAR 64" refers to an article by Mitchell Lynch titled "Hard-Nosing in Academe," published in a journal called *American Way*, in March 1983. This article by Mitchell Lynch in *American Way* is cited by Robert Staples in Staples's article "Racial Ideology and Intellectual Racism: Blacks in Academia," published in *The Black Scholar*, volume 15, beginning on page 2 of the March-April issue, 1984. But the last item on this list turns out to be by the same M. Lynch who wrote the article on "Accommodation Practices." This last reference, "84 UNPUB ART ARTEFACT L," when it's tracked down, turns out to refer to a book by Michael Lynch, *Art and Artefact in Laboratory Science: A Study of Shop Work and Shop Talk in a Research Laboratory*, which was then in press and not published until 1985. Lynch's book is cited in an article by Trevor J. Pinch and Wiebe E. Bijker, "The Social Construction of Facts and Artefacts: Or, How the Sociology of Science and the Sociology of Technology Might Benefit Each Other," published in *Social Studies of Science*, volume 14, beginning on page 399 of the August 1984 issue.

Step Three—Look in the year's *Subject Index* to find articles which have words of interest in their titles. (If you find anything appropriate, then you can find full information about the author[s] in the

Figure 7-4 *Source Index* Entry, *Social Science Citation Index*

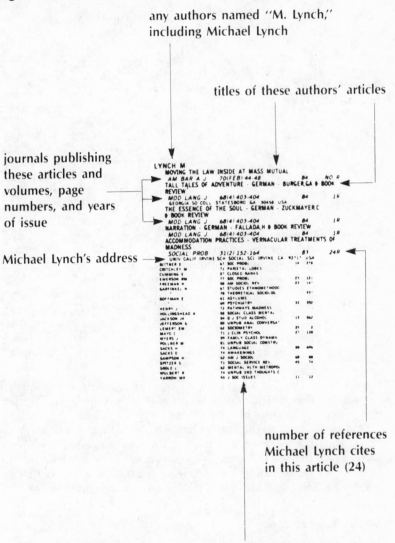

any authors named "M. Lynch,"
including Michael Lynch

titles of these authors' articles

journals publishing
these articles and
volumes, page
numbers, and years
of issue

Michael Lynch's address

number of references
Michael Lynch cites
in this article (24)

information about Michael Lynch's 24 citations (including cited
authors' names, years of publication of cited sources, titles of
cited sources, and volume and beginning page numbers of cited
journal articles)

Figure 7-5   *Citation Index* Entry, *Social Science Citation Index*

any author named "M. Lynch"

dates and titles of
published work
by any M. Lynch

```
LYNCH M
** 1982 83 CURRENT MUNI          9
   KAHN PD        LOC GOVT ST        10     1 84
72 ANN AM ACAD POLIT SS 399     82
   BROMMELS M    HEALTH POLI          4     3 84
75 BRIT MED J    2 127
   NEY PG         CAN J PSY          29    26 84
75 LANCET 7929   317
   SMITH SL       SOC CASE           65   337 84
76 ABUSED CHILD
   RICKEL AU      ADV CL CH P    R    7   295 84
76 ABUSED CHILD MULTIDI
   HOWZE DC       CHILD ABUSE         8   401 84
   MASH EJ        J CLIN CHIL        12   337 83
   TROUT MD       CHILD WELF         62   337 83
76 ABUSED CHILD          43
   OATES RK       ARCH DIS CH        59   147 84
   VESTERDA J     INT J OFFEN        27    21 83
76 S IRELAND NEWSLETTER  11    5
   KEARNS KC      AM J ECON S        43   217 84
77 CHILD ABUSE NEGLECT   1   489
   VESTERDA J     INT J OFFEN        27    21 83
80 Q REV BIOL    55   23
   SEE SCI FOR 5 ADDITIONAL CITATIONS
   BELL MA        COPEIA      N           530 84
81 EDINBURGH REFORMATIO
   COWAN EJ       HIST SOC     B     17   187 84
81 WALL STREET J 0327        54
   ZUICHES JJ     SOCIOL INQ         54   188 84
82 BODY POLITIC NOV        36
   ALTMAN D       SOCIAL REV              93 84
82 EDINBURGH REFORMATIO
   WITHERS CWJ    SCOT GEO M        100    81 84
82 SW U   36 1055
82 SW U   36 1067
   BROWN GD       IA LAW REV         69   617 84
83 AM WAY MAR          61
   SHARP PF       EDUC REC           65    11 84
83 AM WAY MAR          64
   STAPLES R      BLACK SCH          15     2 84
83 W EC ASS
   GRETHER D      ADV CONSUM         11   724 84
83 1983 ANN M CAN SOC A
   SMITH DE       INT SOC SCI        36    59 84
84 COMMUNICATION 0121
   ( ANON )       HARV LAW RE        97  1611 84
84 FORTUNE 110
   WOODRUM VL  FORTUNE       L      110    13 84
84 UNPUB ART ARTEFACT L
   PINCH TJ       SOCIAL ST S        14   399 84
```

other authors who have cited an "M.
Lynch" and titles of the journals
that published these other authors'
work

Source Index, step one.) See Figure 7-6 for an example. From this list
you can tell that M. Lynch used the words "Treatments" and "Vernacular" in a title or titles of his published work.

Step Four—Look in the year's *Corporate Index* to find articles if you
know some corporate or academic institution publishes work on a
topic. From the list in Figure 7-7 you can tell in which journals the
members of the School of Social Sciences at the University of California, Irvine, including M. Lynch, published recent articles.

Social Science Index

This index identifies where and when journal articles on social science topics have been published. The index does not print articles.
Instead, it tells you which issue of the journal to look in for the article
itself. The information is abbreviated, and the abbreviations are explained at the beginning of each volume. You will also find titles of
indexed journals at the beginning of each volume.

Figure 7-6 *Subject Index* Entry, *Social Science Citation Index*

general subject (Madness)

words in titles ⟶
of articles ⟶

The index lists information about articles in two ways, by author's name and by subject headings followed by a list of relevant articles. You can therefore search for information in two ways.

If you know the author's name, look it up in the index by year to see what he or she has published. If you know the year of the publication, simply get the index for that year and look up the author's name. The listings are in alphabetical order. For example, if you are looking for a source citation of an article written by Emerson and Messinger in 1977, pull out the 1977 index and look under Emerson. You will find

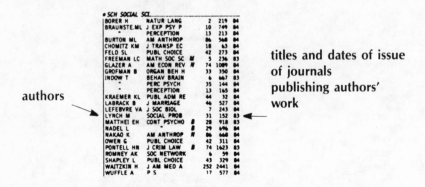

Figure 7-7   *Corporate Index* Entry, *Social Science Citation Index*

CALIFORNIA

IRVINE

institution ——► • UNIV CALIF IRVINE

• SCH SOCIAL SCI

author	journal			
BORER H	NATUR LANG		2	219 84
BRAUNSTE.ML	J EXP PSY P		10	749 84
"	PERCEPTION		13	213 84
BURTON ML	AM ANTHROP		86	568 84
CHOMITZ KM	J TRANSP EC		18	63 84
FELD SL	PUBL CHOICE		42	273 84
FREEMAN LC	MATH SOC SC	N	5	236 83
GLAZER A	AM ECON REV	N	74	1009 84
GROFMAN B	ORGAN BEH H		33	350 84
INDOW T	BEHAV BRAIN		6	667 83
"	PERC PSYCH		35	144 84
"	PERCEPTION		13	165 84
KRAEMER KL	PUBL ADM RE		44	32 84
LABRACK B	J MARRIAGE		46	527 84
LEFEBVRE VA	J SOC BIOL		7	243 84
LYNCH M	SOCIAL PROB		31	152 83
MATTHEI EM	CONT PSYCHO	B	28	918 83
NADEL L	"	B	29	696 84
NAKAO K	AM ANTHROP	N	86	668 84
OWEN G	PUBL CHOICE		42	311 84
PONTELL HN	J CRIM LAW	B	74	1623 83
ROMNEY AK	SOC NETWORK		6	59 84
SHAPLEY L	PUBL CHOICE		43	329 84
WAITZKIN H	J AM MED A		252	2441 84
WUFFLE A	P S		17	577 84

authors

titles and dates of issue
of journals
publishing authors'
work

the information shown in Figure 7-8. This information is abbreviated, and by checking the abbreviations at the beginning of the volume you will be able to establish that Robert M. Emerson and Sheldon L. Messinger published an article, "The Micropolitics of Trouble," on pages 121–134 in volume 25 of the journal *Social Problems*, published in December 1977.

You can also look under subject headings for issues and titles of articles connected with your topic. For example, if you look up "Mentally Ill" in the 1977–78 index, you will find the references to subsections shown in Figure 7-9. By demonstrating a range of topics, the subsections can help you determine which specific aspect of mental illness you are most interested in researching, as well as giving you a sample of references you can begin to read. For example, if you look up the subject heading "Social interaction" in the index, you will find

Figure 7-8   Author's Name, *Social Science Index*

Emerson, Robert M. and Messinger, Sheldon L.
Micro-politics of trouble. bibl Soc Prob 25:121-34 D '77

Figure 7–9   Subject Entry, *Social Science Index*

Mentally ill
   See also
   Aged—Mental illness
   Delinquents—Mental illness
   Emotionally disturbed
   Mental illness
   Mentally handicapped—Mental illness
   Mentally handicapped children—Mental illness
   Neuroses
   Physicians—Mental illness
   Psychiatrists—Mental illness
   Veterans—Mental illness
   Women—Mental illness
   Youth—Mental illness

another reference to this same article, "Micropolitics of Trouble," as shown in Figure 7-10.

International Encyclopedia of the Social Sciences

This source explains key terms and concepts, and provides background information on the life and times of key figures in the history of the social sciences. For example, if you look up the term "alienation," you will find a definition of the term and a discussion of the different ways that Hegel, Marx, and Weber presented this concept in their writings. A bibliography is also given in each entry, but it is not as up-to-date as what you will find in the catalog, abstracts, or indexes.

A Note on Computerized Literature Search

You may be able to take advantage of computer technology to find appropriate bibliographic information. There are two ways students can tap into many data bases, including the reference sources mentioned above. First, your own college library may be able to do a computerized literature search for you. In that case, begin by asking a

Figure 7-10   Subject Entry, *Social Science Index*

Social interaction

Measurement of role identity. P. J. Burke and J. C. Tully. bibl
   Soc Forces 55:881-97 Je '77
Micro-politics of trouble. R. M. Emerson and S. L. Messinger.
   bibl Soc Prob 25:121-34 D '77
Mirroring: one vehicle to organizational clarity. L. Cooper. Int
   J Soc Psych 22:288-95 Wint '76-77

reference librarian about the possibility and cost of this service. Or, second, if you (or your family or dorm) have access to a personal computer and a modem, you can use a commercial online information retrieval service such as Knowledge Index or BRS/After Dark. Again, your own college reference librarian will probably be able to give you information.

A computerized literature search will provide you with a printout listing potential sources that are indexed in a vast network of bibliographical tracking systems. You will then need to sort through the items. Some will be useful and available; others will not. The main advantage of a computerized literature search is its ability to locate a great number of potential sources instantaneously by contacting many different data bases. The disadvantages include cost, getting citations in foreign languages that are not readily available in this country, and not finding important citations in the first place because the keyword descriptors and thesaurus terms used in the search were inappropriate.

Recording Information

Index cards are a handy tool for gathering two kinds of information: bibliographic information on the sources you consult and the ideas you borrow from these sources.

Bibliography cards: Make one bibliography card for each source. Include on this card the following information in this order:

Author: all authors of the work with surnames and first
        names in inverted order
Title: article, chapter, or book
Facts of publication:
        For journals: journal name in full, date of publica-
        tion, volume number, inclusive pages.
        For books: city of publication, publisher's name,
        publication date.

Take this list and the examples with you to the library so that the bibliography cards you write will be complete. You will need all the above information when you cite your sources later in your paper. So write down this information when it's easy to do so, that is, when you have the source in front of you—and avoid wasting valuable time backtracking. Later you will be able to shuffle these bibliography cards into alphabetical order, based on authors' surnames, and in this way prepare the last page(s) of your paper (see Chapter 4). A variation on the note card system is to use a looseleaf binder and looseleaf paper. This allows shuffling and ordering, just as index cards do. Software companies are also beginning to develop and market comparable programs, like "3 × 5," that can be used on a personal computer.

Note cards: You make note cards for two reasons: to support your memory while thinking about a topic and to shape data into usable form. The physical act of recording on cards loads the data into your mind very efficiently, so that you can retrieve them in manageable chunks as you consolidate your own answer to your research question. Note cards also help you avoid problems of parroting and unintentional plagiarism. Parroting means mechanically repeating sources without any sign of your own thinking; for information about the serious offense of plagiarism, see Chapter 5.

Limit each note card to one piece of information from a single article or book. You may quote exact words from the original, or you may paraphrase these ideas. "Paraphrase" means summarize the idea in your own words (see Chapter 5). *Remember to include specific page references* to words and ideas that you record on your note cards as you write them. You will need this information later.

Look for two kinds of information to record on note cards: (1) main concepts related to your research question, and (2) any particularly interesting supporting details. "Interesting" means interesting to you—details that stick in your mind as you read because they connect with your own academic or personal experience.

Label each note card with a subject heading of your own at the top. Try to come up with a description which is precise without copying out the whole note again. You will depend on these subject headings later to group your note cards and sort them into piles. These piles will be the basis for a provisional outline for your paper. At the bottom of each note card, identify the source of your borrowed idea. You can abbreviate this information on a note card because you already have a complete record on a bibliography card. Remember to include the specific page number.

What exactly are you looking for in your note-taking? In some ways, you can think of this part of your work as asking questions not unlike those you would pose in a textual analysis (see Chapter 6). Your notes should indicate answers to the key questions about the article or book you are reading: What major question is the author addressing in this work? Why does the author think the question is important to sociological theory or to the world at large? What methods did the researchers use to try to answer the question and/or what work of others is cited to make a significant point? What thesis does the author propose in response to the question? What evidence does he or she use to support the answer?

As you take notes you will see that there is no one answer to your research question. It is not a matter of finding the truth, but of tracing the main issues raised in regard to the question, the main answers proposed, and the main disagreements among those engaged in the field. Eventually you will use these notes to explain in your paper why you believe one answer to be more convincing than the others which have been suggested.

When you first start your project you may find yourself making quite a few note cards because the subject is often new to you. However, as you read more, and become more informed, you will be narrowing down the answer to your question. At the same time your thesis will be emerging more clearly in your own mind, and you will be selecting subsequent readings more deliberately. As the material becomes familiar you will likely take fewer notes per reading. This process of adjustment and refinement happens almost automatically.

Here is an original passage from Emile Durkheim's book *Suicide* (1951:168); Figure 7-11 shows one sample note card based on the passage:

> As a rule suicide increases with knowledge. Knowledge does not determine this progress. It is innocent; nothing is more unjust than to accuse it.... But these two facts result simultaneously from a single general state which they translate into different forms. Man seeks to learn and man kills himself because of the loss of cohesion in his religious society; he does not kill himself because of his learning. It is certainly not the learning he acquires that disorganizes religion; but the desire for knowledge wakens because religion becomes disorganized. Knowledge is not sought as a means to destroy accepted opinions but because their destruction has commenced.

Remember to include on your note cards the page number(s) of quotations and paraphrased ideas. Otherwise you may later have to skim the entire source just to locate the page for a passage you want to cite.

Looking Deeper

Now that you are immersed in your topic, you can use the materials that you have found to direct you to further books and articles which may be useful to you. As you are engaged in taking notes, make bibliographical cards for any references in your reading which seem relevant to your topic. You may discover these in the body of the work itself or in the References at the end. The catalog (for books) and serials list (for periodical literature such as journal articles) will help you again in locating these references in your library.

Figure 7-11   Example of a Note Card

Subject heading label
identifying noted idea

Borrowed idea recorded as
part quotation/
part paraphrase

Bibliographic information
identifying source

Organizing Your Information

Once you have finished making note cards, reread them in any order
to get an overview of your information. You should now be able to
state your thesis, which these notes support, very clearly. With your
thesis in mind, sort your note cards into piles, according to the subject headings you gave them. This shuffling will not necessarily be
neat, but you will be distinguishing separate main points and preparing the basis for an outline.

Matching Thesis, Note Cards, and Outline

Decide on the main point in each pile of note cards and make that a
main point on an outline. Use the detailed information in the pile to
elaborate this main point.

You may find that some of your note cards no longer fit the final version of your thesis. If so, abandon them. Including irrelevant information, even though you worked hard to get it, will distract your reader, weaken your argument, and count against you.

In order to decide on a sequence of main points—that is, which main point to start with and what order to follow with the others— think of your reader. What order will be the most convincing? What order of main points will best support your thesis? Then use each main point as the basis of a different paragraph. Use details from your piles of note cards to build up each paragraph, presenting your sequence of thoughts in a logical pattern with transitions marking the movement of your argument (see Chapter 10 for more information on transitions). In the concluding section, summarize your major findings. Here you can also briefly refer to other related issues or topics that merit further investigation.

Major Journals Often Used by Sociologists

Scholars rely on journal articles, as well as books, to keep up with new research and professional opinion. But journals aren't a trade secret. Undergraduates, who are apprentice scholars, can also use them. Most college libraries have a special quiet, convenient place where current issues of major journals are kept before being bound and shelved, like other books, in the main sections of the library. We recommend that you find this reading area, often called "Current Periodicals," and browse through some of the journals listed below. This experience will give you a dramatic sense of the discipline's ongoing research tradition, which is only hinted at in textbooks. It may also trigger some ideas about possible topics for your own future papers. Although the articles in these journals are intended primarily for a trained scholarly audience, rather than the general public, and sometimes employ sophisticated statistical techniques, you will find many articles easily accessible to undergraduates.

American Journal of Sociology: Published bimonthly by the University of Chicago Press, this influential journal includes theoretical and research articles, book reviews, and commentaries on articles published previously.

American Sociological Review: Published bimonthly by the American Sociological Association (ASA), this review covers diverse areas of sociology, often with a statistical and empirical orientation. A cumulative index appears every three years.

Annual Review of Sociology: These review articles, which summarize some particular field of sociology, reflect a broad perspective and can be found under such categories as differentiation and stratification, institutions, political and economic sociology, social processes, policy, historical sociology, urban sociology, and political sociology.

British Journal of Sociology: Published quarterly, this journal discusses historical and theoretical as well as methodological issues. An annual index also includes book reviews.

Contemporary Sociology: Published bimonthly by the ASA, its special feature is to review books, journals, articles, and films, covering a wide range of areas such as historical and comparative sociology, social psychology, gender, education, and stratification. The review essays are especially useful for learning about new publications and sociologists' evaluations of them.

Criminology: Published quarterly, this interdisciplinary journal emphasizes research about crime and deviant behavior within the social and behavioral sciences and presents articles on the theoretical and historical components of crime, law, and criminal justice.

Journal of Contemporary Ethnography: Published quarterly, it presents ethnographic studies based on qualitative interviewing and participant observation.

Journal of Health and Social Behavior: Published quarterly by the ASA, it uses a sociological perspective in understanding health-related issues, for example, organizational aspects of hospitals or class characteristics of sufferers from various illnesses.

Journal of Marriage and the Family: Published quarterly by the National Council on Family Relations, it covers such diverse research areas as family planning, family structure, theories of the family, and cross-cultural studies on fertility. Each issue also features a book review section.

Social Forces: Published quarterly, this journal for social research and methodology presents articles on such topics as mobility, class, ethnicity, gender, and education. Each issue includes book reviews.

Social Problems: Published five times yearly, this is the official journal of the Society for the Study of Social Problems.

Social Psychology Quarterly: Published quarterly by the ASA, it covers empirical and theoretical studies related to social interaction, socialization, labeling, conformity, and attitudes.

Social Science Quarterly: It features book reviews, forums, research notes, and articles concerned with social issues, including such topics as race and ethnicity, family migration, and criminology.

Sociological Inquiry: Published quarterly for the chapters of the Alpha Kappa Delta (the Undergraduate Sociology Honors Society), it covers a wide range of sociological topics.

Sociological Methods and Research: Published quarterly, it covers research in methodological, quantitative, and empirical issues in the field of sociology, and also includes review articles.

Sociological Quarterly: This journal presents research on recent theoretical, methodological, and empirical developments in the field of sociology.

Sociological Review: Published quarterly in England, this interdisciplinary journal presents a range of sociological topics such as social mobility and class structure, and includes book reviews.

Sociological Theory: A semiannual publication of the American Sociological Association, it is devoted to discussions of new and old sociological theories, theory construction, and theory synthesis. The journal also includes a section for debate and comment on recent theoretical controversies.

Sociology and Social Research: Published quarterly, this journal's interdisciplinary approach is reflected in its research articles, review articles, and book reviews.

Symbolic Interaction: Published semiannually by the Society for the Study of Symbolic Interaction, this specialized journal presents empirical and theoretical articles which take a symbolic interactionist perspective.

This list is not exhaustive. For more references to specialized journals and governmental sources, ask your reference librarian or consult

Bart, Pauline and Linda Frankel
    1986   The Student Sociologist's Handbook. 4th ed. New York:
              Random House.

Chapter 8

THE ETHNOGRAPHIC FIELD RESEARCH PAPER

In an ethnographic field research project, your data come from observing or interacting with people in everyday social settings, which are known as the "the field." The data are gathered through observation when a researcher visits the setting, participates in the setting's activities ("participant observation"), and/or interviews participants in the setting.

Goals and Methods of Ethnographic Field Research

1. Ethnographic field research sets out to represent as accurately as possible the process of social life *from the point of view of the participants* (or "members") in the field setting being investigated. Since a scientific hypothesis is an explanation of social processes proposed by someone *outside* the research setting, the ethnographic researcher does not engage in hypothesis-testing. In other words, ethnographic field research generally follows an *inductive* model of research (see Chapter 1).

Some sociologists engage in fieldwork as part of a *deductive* research process to test hypotheses about what happens in social settings or why. This kind of fieldwork, which we will refer to as "structured field research," is discussed in Chapter 9.

2. The ethnographic researcher usually conducts research by closely observing what people are doing, talking to them informally, and often participating in activities with them. If interviews are conducted, the ethnographer uses questions that encourage respondents to answer in their own ways and with their own words. The choice of

methods used in ethnographic research depends on the characteristics of the setting and its inhabitants and on the personal style of the researcher.

Unlike most deductive researchers, then, the ethnographic field researcher does not use a predesigned research instrument, such as a written questionnaire. And, unlike the structured fieldwork described in Chapter 9, ethnographic field research rarely involves quantitative measurement. While predesigned and quantitative methods are useful for measuring some aspects of the social world, they do not convey the intricate and subtle transactions which the ethnographer seeks to understand.

3. Reports based on ethnographic field research—called "ethnographies"—often produce new theoretical insights, but they are most distinctive for their vivid descriptions of actual social scenes and transactions. In other words, even after collecting data, the ethnographer typically does not attempt to propose a hypothesis about *why* something happens in the social world. Instead, ethnographic research attempts to uncover *what* happens in a social setting, *how* social relationships are conducted, and what those events and relationships mean to those involved.

In doing ethnographic research, your sociological imagination is exercised by the opportunity to see society's institutions, such as the police, the judicial system, or the health care system, as they are actually enacted in the personal lives of specific individuals. Because it takes sociology out of the classroom and into the "real world," and because it allows you to view the world through the eyes of people often very different from yourself, an ethnographic field research project can be especially challenging and exciting.

Asking an Appropriate Question

Often the goal of your research project will be specified by your instructor. Ethnographic research assignments frequently ask you to do one of the following:

1. Look at social interaction in your everyday life—among family, friends, fellow students, co-workers, for example—in new ways. The goals are to describe patterns and processes which often pass unnoticed in your daily interactions and to use your sociological imagination to relate these personal patterns and processes to specific course concepts. This kind of project might ask you, for instance, to talk to fellow students about their relationships with friends; observe how those in your dorm, apartment, or family deal with odd behavior; or

watch how individuals attempt to present a certain impression of themselves to others.

2. Visit a setting selected by your instructor, in which social activities of special concern in your course occur, and investigate how those present carry out routine activities and make decisions. Examples of this kind of assignment are going on a police ride-along, attending traffic or small claims court, or interviewing a mental health professional.

In some classes, however, you may have to develop your own question to address through ethnographic research, or you may simply be assigned to visit a setting of your choice and describe what it is like. If so, remember that, unlike much other sociological research, the goal of ethnographic field research is not to determine what causes some social event or relationship. Therefore, avoid devising a research question that asks *why* something happens in your research setting. Instead, concentrate on asking *"what"* (for example, "What does a police officer do during his or her time on the job?") or *"how"* (for example, "How do those sharing an elevator ride deal with one another in the limited space available?") In the sample student paper at the end of this chapter, the author addresses a "how" question: "How do family members react when a relative exhibits odd or unpredictable behavior?"

Here are the kinds of "what" and "how" questions that will point your ethnographic research in the right direction: What do people do in this setting? How do they explain what they do? What kinds of things interest and concern them? How do group members work together to accomplish a task? How are new members taught the values and procedures common to the setting? What do group members mean by any special words they use?

Reviewing the Literature

In a deductive research process, a review of relevant research done on the same topic is used to develop a hypothesis for testing through data collection. However, because the kind of fieldwork we are describing here does not involve hypothesis-testing, instructors assigning ethnographic research projects often do not require that you summarize the literature on the question you are investigating.

Nevertheless, your instructor, in order to encourage you to become familiar with work already done on the question you are investigating, may prefer that you give an overview of relevant research on your subject. Or you yourself may find a literature review useful in getting

a feel for ethnographic research, in choosing a setting or a question
for your research, or in understanding the issues of concern to those
you will be observing in the field. In this case, use the guidelines in
Chapter 7 to get an overview of the sociological literature relevant to
your project.

Collecting Your Data

Understand the Assignment

Where are you supposed to go? What are you to look for? Are you
expected mainly to present your own reactions or to describe what
others do in the setting? Is the task to demonstrate your ability to
apply course concepts to what you see, to provide a detailed account
of interaction in the observed settings, or both? Is there a specific
question you should address?

Plan Ahead

1. Begin early in the quarter or semester. Field data cannot always be
collected predictably or on short notice. Furthermore, you may have
to return to your field setting several times to get the additional information or understanding that you need. Your time grid (see Chapter 2) can help you allot the time you will need.

2. Make arrangements to interview or observe. While the prospect
of getting permission may make you anxious at first, you will find
that most people are receptive to showing you or telling you about
their lives. You can assure them that their identities will remain con-
fidential if the information is personal. Be sure to follow the procedures established by your college's Human Subjects and Ethics
Committee, which might require you to submit your research plan for
approval or to obtain written permission from those you observe or
interview; consult your instructor for details.

When scheduling your observation or interview, allow plenty of
time. Unanticipated events may occur, your subject may begin to talk
at length about some particularly interesting topic, or you may think
of additional questions on the spot. Also, you will need time to record,
transcribe, or elaborate on notes immediately after the contact.

3. Plan how you will record your data (see the next section for a
summary of recording options). In interview situations, it is best to
tape record or to make notes during the interview. Likewise, notes
made while observing are more reliable than those made after you've
left your field setting. The methods you choose will depend on the

situation and your personal style. But, whatever approach you take, be prepared ahead of time with adequate supplies of audio tape, batteries, paper, and pencil, as appropriate.

Observe the Setting

Although you may know a lot about the setting and the interactions you observe, it is crucial that you leave behind your previous assumptions and even your knowledge about them, in order to learn something new. Adopt the attitude of a naive outsider so that you can begin to look in a new way at events and experiences you used to take for granted. In other words, don't try to figure out beforehand what conclusions you should come to, or how you will use the information you are collecting. Just be as attentive to detail as you can so you can get as much valuable information as possible.

When observing: Don't presume you know which events or interactions matter most. Keep your eyes and ears open to everything that is going on around you. Notice your surroundings, all the people who are present, the time taken by events, and so on. Attempt, above all, to look at the setting or situation through the eyes of participants.

When interviewing:

1. Don't talk more than you have to. Listen carefully to the respondent.

2. Avoid leading questions which define the respondent's answer, and avoid questions that point to yes or no answers.

3. Rather than asking why something happened, concentrate on asking how it occurred. "Why" questions often put people on the defensive, making them feel forced to justify their actions or life-style. Also, respondents' answers to "how" questions will be more specific about real events, providing you with the concrete examples you need to describe in detail what goes on in the setting.

4. Don't overwhelm your interviewee with multiple questions. If you are a new interviewer, you may be especially sensitive to silence, but don't rush in with comments, clarification, or further questions if the respondent pauses. Allow the respondent time to think and time to complete his or her response fully.

5. Encourage the respondent to be fairly specific about the details of events or experiences: Exactly who was involved? What happened? When did it take place? Remember, however, that probing should be gentle (for example, "Could you tell me more about that?"), not an interrogation.

6. Relax, allow your natural curiosity about your subject to direct you, and LISTEN.

Record Your Data

Since the final paper you produce will be only as good as your recorded data, it is crucial that you record observations or interview responses accurately, in detail, as soon as possible after the event. Otherwise, you will inevitably forget or distort what was said or done.

In observational research, take notes on what you see or hear as it happens. If that is impossible or bothers those you are observing, then record what you observed as soon as possible afterward. You may even want to take periodic "note-taking breaks" away from the setting during your observation to jot down a few words or phrases which will trigger your memory later.

If you are interviewing, it is best to tape the conservation. Don't be shy about asking permission to tape or take notes during the interview. People are often agreeable, once they understand your interest in accurately representing what they say.

If subjects seem reluctant to let you tape, don't force the issue. Just listen to their responses and reconstruct the interview in writing as soon as you can afterward. Don't editorialize in your reporting of what was said. Likewise, don't edit your interview to make responses seem more sensible or because something seems "inconsequential." If you edit or editorialize, you may leave out something significant. Report all the respondent's comments, keeping them in their original order. And be sure to include all your questions, as well as the answers to them.

If you do tape an interview, it will be helpful to transcribe it into written form. There are special dictation machines that make transcription easier. Or, at the least, you should listen carefully to the interview and take notes on both your questions and the responses.

In all cases, make your notes specific. Describe in detail what you observed, did, and/or heard. Like a good reporter, give the specifics of who, what, when, and where. Include concrete details about the physical setting, what went on, and your reactions: how did you feel about the people with whom you were involved? Remember that in ethnographic field research you are the research instrument; it is through your person, your interactions, and your relations that you learn about the people and settings you are studying. For that reason, your personal reactions are especially important.

You may be required to submit the originals, or a typed version, of your field notes as an appendix to your paper. Or you might choose to include your notes in an appendix, in order to give your instructor a better appreciation of what happened in your setting or interview (and of how hard you worked to gather your data!). Even if you will not be submitting your notes, keep them legible and organized. Be sure, for example, to date every entry. The quality of your paper relies on the quality of your field notes; the more clear data you have available, the stronger your paper will be.

Example of Observational Field Notes

Here are sample observational and interview notes to give you an idea of general format and content.

The following is an excerpt written up by a student in an introductory ethnography class, based on field notes jotted down while observing. The assignment asked students to observe interactions in public settings. The student chose to observe a familiar scene that was part of her everyday life.

OUR COMMENTS

Unlike your final paper, which should be double-spaced, it is usually okay to single-space your field notes. However, be sure to leave wide margins, for comments (your own or the instructor's) and coding.

It's perfectly normal to be nervous about entering a new situation. Take a deep breath and try to relax. Like the subjects in these notes, many people being observed are quite friendly and very willing to talk about their work.

We all have assumptions about other people and the world we live in. What is challenging and fun about sociology is the opportunity to get past those assumptions and learn new ways of seeing things. Remember to keep an open mind.

Observation #3: Bus Riding

With considerable trepidation, I boarded the bus to
campus with the intention of speaking to bus drivers about
their perceptions of bus riding and their role in it.
Previous observations had led me to the conclusion that bus
drivers were either identified with, or detached from, their
roles so much that their attitudes and behaviors were very
brusque and "macho." The first of many such assumptions was
shot down as I discovered that today's driver on my route was
a young Hispanic woman of slight build: hardly the burly type
at all! I approached her after everyone else had left the bus
at the campus terminal. I introduced myself, told her that I
would like to ask her a few questions about her job for a
class assignment. She said that she liked her job, that "it's
great if you like driving!", but that she had just a few
minutes. I asked her if I could wait at the terminal for her
after my class and ride the entire route with her. She said

Whenever possible, make a note right away of direct quotations. Otherwise, paraphrase as accurately as possible.

Notice how the drivers all keep looking at their watches! It's important to note as many little details as possible, even if you can't recall them all completely. This early observation, about the bus driver's precision about time, turned out to be a major theme in the field notes: through her observation, the author of these notes came to appreciate the rhythm of the bus driver's workday and the memory skill it takes to do his or her job.

The question about how people "click off" on the bus is too directive. It doesn't produce much useful information. Contrast it to the more open-ended question below, about what the *subject* thinks is the most outstanding feature about bus-riding.

Remember that your notes are not a formal treatise. Describe gesture, sounds, even smells, through whatever means necessary to bring the setting or conversation alive.

What did the subjects *do* that led the observer to believe they were preoccupied or hurried?

In many ways, you already have much practice at entering new social settings. Use your everyday conversational skills to make contact with your subject—they're "just people" too!

sure, and explained a process I didn't completely understand
about how she would be replaced at 4th and Colorado at
11-something that morning, for a lunch break, but would be
back on the route later, and her "last run of the day" left
UCLA at 3-something. I agreed I would wait on campus until
her later run passed through. What struck me most was how
precisely she knew the route and schedule: "Fourth and
Colorado" had such exactness, and sounded so familiar to her;
both times she mentioned about the schedule were to the
minute, and were from memory. As I stood to leave, she
glanced at her watch.

I sat on the stairs which lead down to the bus terminal
after class that afternoon. I figured I might have a wait of
up to an hour and that I might as well try to work up the
nerve to talk to the drivers who hang around on the stairs
between runs, or who go up them to get a snack on campus. One
driver I was familiar with from riding his route walked
downstairs and commented that I had found a "good seat, out
of the sun." I told him I was observing bus riding. He said
it [bus riding] is "very interesting" and that I should "take
a notebook or a tape recorder along on a ride." I asked if
he'd ever noticed something I'd observed, that people seem to
"click off" while on the bus, almost like they're not really
there. "Oh, sure, well some get sick on the bus, so they do
other things. That's why you hear the 'bzz-bzz' [the
stop-the-bus signal] so much. They suddenly [he mimes
someone becoming alert, looking around—indicating someone
realizing where they are]." He'd been pausing, moving slowly
down the last few steps, now glanced at his watch, quickened
his pace, gestured in a wave, and returned to his bus.

There were a few other drivers coming and going, but I
didn't initiate any conversation. Some seemed hurried, some
preoccupied. One, however, was walking downstairs with a
snack. I commented that he'd gotten himself a treat. He said,
"I'm starving. I haven't had time to get something to eat." I
told him I was sorry I'd finished my banana already, or I'd
be happy to share it. We agreed on the ribsticking virtues of
bananas. [Food: the universal bond!] I told him I was
observing bus-riding for a class. He smiled. "That

Notice how important the inclusion of the driver's "chuckle" is. Without noting it, it would be hard to tell whether he is being sarcastic or funny or what. Don't trust your memory to remind you. Even though it's obvious at the time, it's easy to forget when you observe many settings and talk to a number of people.

Notice the results of asking the subject what is outstanding (or interesting or unusual or important) about the setting *from his or her point of view!* An issue is raised which the observer had never considered, but which is central to the experience of bus driving. Much more information could have been elicited, however, by probing for details with "what" and "how" questions: *how* did the person try to get around paying the fare; *how* did the the driver outsmart the two riders who wanted to avoid buying transfers; *what* excuses do people offer for not having the money?

[bus—riding] is really interesting. [Chuckle] Yep, that's
really interesting." I asked what feature he thought was most
outstanding about bus—riding. He said I should see the number
of ways people try to avoid paying. I indicated surprise,
since I'd never observed this. He assured me it was common,
and described a few instances—one person who tried to just
get out of paying the 25—cent fare, two guys who tried to
avoid having to buy transfers (and how he outsmarted them),
the ways people give excuses for not having the money.

COMMENTS ON EXAMPLE OF INTERVIEW NOTES

The "interviewer" in this example was effective in a number of ways:

1. She uses "what" and "how" questions to elicit information from her subject. The focus is not on "why" the father was acting oddly, but on how it was dealt with in family interactions.

2. She uses open-ended questions, allowing the subject to describe behaviors and events in her own terms. None of the questions asked could have been answered with a simple yes or no.

3. In the third question, she probes for a specific example. Such concrete events allow you to describe behavior and settings in specific terms.

Example of Interview Notes

The following is a brief example of the kind of interview notes, transcribed from audio tape, that Sandra Ducoff Garber might have used to develop her paper on accommodation practices.

Sandra: How did your family respond to your father's odd behavior?

Sally: He really bugged me. It got to the point where I couldn't stand to deal with him at all. I did the standard trick of look at his ear and not at his face which just drove him up the wall and he would get so frustrated and so angry. That just made him madder, of course, but I didn't care. I just couldn't handle it. He made *me* so mad.

Sandra: What were some other ways you or other family members dealt with the trouble he was causing?

Sally: My mother got really weird about it, kind of pretending nothing was wrong.

Sandra: Can you tell me about a specific time she did that?

Sally: Well, one time my mother and sister were driving in the Loop and saw my father staggering drunk on a busy street in the Loop. And my mother said to my sister, "My God, it's your father! Get him in the car!" So, my sister pushed him into the car and my mother drove off and went on talking as if nothing had happened.

Organizing Your Data

The observations and answers you collect in your fieldwork are the data on which your paper will be based. In this step of your research process, you use the material which you have collected to answer the question which your instructor assigned or which you formulated. This is an exciting process, because, as you look back over your notes, you will notice that the setting you have learned about in a personal way reveals interesting information about the nature of social life.

Answering an Assigned Question

If your instructor asked a specific question in your paper assignment, now is the time to consider how what you saw, heard, and experienced addresses the question. Here are some guidelines, followed by an illustration using the sample ethnographic field research paper which follows this chapter:

1. Go through your notes and make a mark by every comment, observation, or response that seems relevant to the question being asked. Don't be too discriminating at this point. Better to include too much at this stage than too little.

2. Copy these relevant pieces of data onto separate note cards, or photocopy your original notes and from the photocopy cut and paste the relevant excerpts onto the cards; this will allow you to lay the bits of data out side by side, much as you would for materials in a library research paper (see Chapter 7). Note that you should *never* cut up your original notes. Always save your original and use a photocopy or carbon for cutting. Also be sure to indicate on each card the page number of your field notes from which the excerpt was taken, so that you can include the citation if you quote the excerpt in your paper.

3. Now consider what the information on each card says in response to the question asked in the assignment. What does it tell you about the setting you observed and/or the people you interviewed?

4. Look for patterns among your cards. Move them around to illustrate to yourself how the information fits together. For instance, you might stack together cards which contain examples of the same kind of behavior. Or you might arrange appropriate cards to reflect stages in a process.

Course materials and the paper assignment itself may be useful in helping you notice the patterns in your data. Recall concepts covered in the class which are relevant to your project. Review carefully just what the assignment directs you to look at. Then consider how your data illustrate those concepts or teach you something about the social relations you observed.

For instance, Sandra Ducoff Garber, the student author of the sample ethnographic paper which follows this chapter, was asked by the instructor of her course on the sociology of mental illness to describe "the ways some particular social group . . . manage their activities so as to continue to live/work with another who is making difficulties for them." In the class, the instructor had lectured and assigned reading on various strategies which groups adopt for maintaining relationships with a troublesome member.

In analyzing her interview notes, Sandra might well have listed these strategies and then stacked in separate piles excerpts from her data which illustrated each of these strategies. Or, since she chose to tell the story of her subject's family chronologically, she might have organized her notes according to the stages which seem relevant from the subject's point of view: before age eight through junior high school; from junior high through high school; and as a young adult. With her cards ordered in these stages, Sandra could then consider how the family's definition of the problem and their response to it differed from stage to stage.

Answering a Broader Question

Perhaps you were simply assigned (or chose as your project) to participate in and describe a social setting. It will still be useful to sort out excerpts from your notes as described above, but you will probably have more freedom to establish the categories into which you will organize your observations.

Begin by carefully rereading your field notes to refresh your memory about the events. Then start to look for patterns in your notes. As in the case of an assigned question, you might use course concepts to organize this search. Better yet, you might try to find the categories and terms used by people you observed, asking yourself how *they* understand and describe their activities.

For example, if you were taking a course in deviant behavior, your text would probably spend considerable space defining "deviance" in terms of breaking social norms. But in ethnographic research you would find that the people you observe don't talk about "deviance" or "norms." Thus, rather than looking in your notes for examples of what your text would define as "deviance," it would be more enlightening to pinpoint what specific behaviors your subjects perceive as odd or disruptive and to note the ways in which they categorize and describe those who exhibit disliked behavior (such as referring to them as "weird" or as "different from us"). Similarly, a course in stratification may present sophisticated ways of measuring socioeconomic status; but, since the most interesting and valuable findings-from your ethnographic field research concern the ways in which the people you observe perceive their own position in relation to society, you might look through your notes for all the ways they compare themselves to other groups.

Some of the most common themes ethnographers look for include the ways members characterize their group; the ways they distinguish between insiders and outsiders; the special language they develop to describe their shared activities and values; their patterns of interaction; the ways they teach new members the ropes; the ways they identify and respond to behavior they don't like; the ways in which members experience their setting through the course of an event, a workday, or any other unit of experience. You may find some or all of these reflected in your notes and you may find interesting themes not listed here. You may choose to focus on one area or on several related themes.

As you begin to identify themes that run through your field notes, you can proceed to sort the excerpts into piles, as described in the section above.

Writing Your Paper

Because ethnographic field research does not involve hypothesis-testing, the essay format discussed in Chapter 1 is more appropriate for your paper than the journal format. Simply modify it slightly: in place of the three (or more) "claims" or "points" relevant to a paper which proposes and supports a thesis, substitute the themes or concepts which you identified in your field notes. These will serve as the body of your paper. Even though an ethnography does not always propose an answer and attempt to prove why it is more "accurate," remember that you are responsible for demonstrating, through effective use of your data, why your description of the setting is believable. Be sure to describe your research methods—where you went, how long you stayed, to whom you spoke, and so on—and to include as evidence the most illustrative excerpts from your field notes.

If the question you are addressing was assigned, you can use one of two approaches to present a written report on your observations:

First, you can describe what happened or what was said, chronologically, and comment on how course concepts apply to the things you describe, as you report them in the order in which they occurred. This is the strategy employed in the sample paper which follows this chapter.

Second, you can organize your paper around concepts, defining and indicating the importance of each, and using your data to illustrate them. In this case, you can follow the essay format, taking for each of your main points a selected concept or group of concepts.

Unless your assignment specifically requires one approach, either can be successful. If you are uncertain which approach to take, or which may be preferred, discuss your plans with your instructor. In either case, return to course concepts and themes frequently. Ask yourself how the events or comments you are describing reflect or illustrate sociological ideas. This will help you avoid the common mistake of making overly psychological interpretations of those whom you observe or interview.

If your assignment didn't specify a particular question for you to answer or a specific setting for you to analyze according to course concepts, then you can simply organize the themes you discovered in your notes into the essay format. You might choose three points to make about one of the themes that you found most interesting or revealing. Or, you might develop your paper around three different themes.

Whichever format you use, it is important for your paper to incorporate the reactions you experienced in your research and recorded in your notes. Inevitably, those engaged in ethnographic field research encounter people, events, and experiences which fascinate, surprise, confuse, or even upset them. It is a challenge to make effective use of such reactions without getting sidetracked into self-analysis. A good way to make your personal reactions relevant is to ask yourself what they illuminate about the setting. Describe in your paper the ways in which your own feelings and thoughts helped you better understand the people whom you studied and their interactions.

When writing your paper, you may quote your field notes directly. When you do, punctuate and cite them as you would any other source. Or you may choose to summarize an incident or a response in an anecdotal way to illustrate a point. As long as they are relevant to your assignment, use your collected data in as many ways as you can; they make up the empirical basis for your discussion.

Suggested Reading

Emerson, Robert M.
    1983   *Contemporary Field Research: A Collection of Readings.* Boston: Little, Brown.
Van Maanen, John
    1988   *Tales of the Field: On Writing Ethnography.* Chicago: University of Chicago Press.

A Sample Student Paper

Our sample paper illustrating ethnographic field research was written by Sandra Ducoff Garber for a class in the sociology of mental illness in the fall of 1985. It responds to an assigned question: "How does some particular social group—a family, dorm hall, a living group, a work group—manage their activities so as to continue to live/work with another who is making difficulties for them?" The ethnographic method Sandra chose was to interview a woman about her family experiences. Her title, "The Purpose of Accommodation Practices in the Family: A Case Study," and her introduction alert us that she examined a family's "accommodation practices," that is, members' strategies for coping "with a father whose behavior was disruptive of the lives of the other family members" (paragraph 3). Thus, the theme around which she organized the paper is drawn from the course assignment.

Sandra's essay presents this theme chronologically—how this family coped with the father at different periods in their family history. Notice that she consistently makes connections between concepts drawn from the course and empirical data collected during the interview. Her interpretations are supported by examples from her notes. Our comments on the paper point out in more detail how she has used her data to construct her paper.

Sandra's conclusion reflects her sociological imagination by showing how the interactions of one family illustrate strategies used by many social groups, including other families faced with similar challenges.

THE PURPOSE OF ACCOMMODATION PRACTICES IN THE FAMILY:

A CASE STUDY

Sandra Ducoff Garber
Sociology 157
Professor Melvin Pollner
December 6, 1985

Because of the length of Sandra's paper, she has included a title page, following
most of the correct format (see Chapter 11). She should not have capitalized every
word in the title, however.

113

OUR COMMENTS

Sandra's first paragraph adopts a sociological perspective by connecting her topic to social interaction and deviance.

Here she briefly reviews course materials which will be relevant to her paper.

Sandra makes it clear early in the paper how she has gone about completing the assignment: her field research consisted of interviewing an individual about how family members dealt with the father's disruptive behavior.

The introduction stimulates the reader's interest by offering a preview of some interesting findings.

The usual methods of social interaction are generally inadequate for dealing with an individual who communicates and acts in ways beyond the symbols, assumptions, and understandings of his group. As long as the group is maintained with the aberrant person as part of it, other methods must be developed (Pollner, 1985).

These alternative methods of interaction have various purposes as well as forms. Edwin Lemert's "Paranoia and the Dynamics of Exclusion" (1962) studied the ways in which co-workers isolated and disempowered someone with a certain type of obnoxious behavior in the workplace. Marian Yarrow et al., in "The Psychological Meaning of Mental Illness in the Family" (1955), described the strategies of a number of wives in interpreting their husbands' odd behavior with the goal of accepting it and continuing their partnership. Michael Lynch (1983) presented and defined a large assortment of accommodation practices reported by students, mostly in coping with someone behaving oddly in their living spaces. He concluded that the accommodation practices served the group to create a "semblance of normal individuality for troublemakers" (1983:162). Presumably that semblance of normality is then extended to the groups that contain the troublemaker.

In this paper I am examining the strategies of members of a family who were trying to cope with a father whose behavior was disruptive of the lives of other family members, and who had effectively abdicated most of the responsibilities of his role as father in the family. The subject of my interview was the oldest daughter, the second child out of seven. Her description of the family dynamics indicated a very different function for the coping strategies of the children from that of their mother.

When Sally, the daughter, was eight years old, her father suffered a series of increases in financial responsibility at the same time a reorganization at his job made him very unhappy there. Three of his children became seriously ill, a purchase of some property tied up all his money, and a fifth child was born. The deterioration of his relationship with the family was gradual, but the children

Sandra could be more specific here regarding what incidents led family members to believe that their roles "had to be maintained." Also, the phrase "the implications of anyone's actual behavior" is unclear.

Here Sandra shows how the situation she is investigating illustrates concepts which have been presented in class.

Note how her interview notes are used as evidence, just as materials from a book or article might be.

Sandra accurately and appropriately applies the concept of "denial" as a way of dealing with disruptive behavior, as it was presented in the course.

were aware of their father coming home from work each night
expressing more and more anger by shouting and hissing at the
television, lecturing the children obsessively on theology
and what they felt to be inane topics, and drinking more and
more.

The parents were strictly and devoutly Catholic. The
father's authoritarian role along with the mother's
supportive and mediating role and the children's role of
obedience and unquestioning respect, all had to be maintained
regardless of the implications of anyone's actual behavior or
feelings. The members of the family did not communicate with
each other nor with anyone outside about what was going on.
The children came to avoid any communication with their
father partly as a way to "limit the gross possibility of
interaction" (Lynch, 1983:155) and partly because they found
that their ignoring him upset him.

> I did the standard trick of look [sic] at his ear and
> not at his face which just drove him up the wall and he
> would get so frustrated and so angry.

It was to the children an acceptable way to express their
anger.

By accepting her religion's concept of her role, the
mother felt absolutely prohibited from leaving the situation
or even from exerting any real pressure on her husband to
modify his behavior. Therefore, she "denied" (Yarrow et
al., 1955) her husband's outrageous behavior by refusing to
acknowledge it.

> One time my mother and sister were driving in the Loop
> and saw my father staggering drunk on a busy street in
> the Loop. And my mother said to my sister, "My God,
> it's your father! Get him in the car!" So, my sister
> pushed him into the car and my mother drove off and went
> on talking as if nothing had happened.

She was also anxious to preserve appearances and, when a
neighbor commented on the fact that the husband frequently
was heard driving away in the middle of the night, the mother
explained that "driving at night relaxed him."

Sandra uses her interview notes well. Here we can see why field research can be so rewarding, as real life examples make sociological concepts more interesting.

Here Sandra demonstrates a key point covered in class: because family life is a set of relationships from which members cannot easily escape, they must develop ways of coping with a member's disruptive behaviors.

Sandra might have commented here on the identification of the father as "sick" since the course materials focus on how those affected by troublesome behavior come to attach such a label to it.

More serious to the children were the times when she
"covered for" him (Lynch, 1983:160) regarding his behavior
toward them.

> One night he really scared me . . . I was out sleeping
> in the living room and he came up to me and he started
> saying he loved me and kissing me all over my face and
> my neck and I remember being really scared. . . . But at
> the same time, this was my dad; this was an authority
> figure; you don't push this person away. But I kind of
> did a little bit and he left very abruptly. . . . So,
> very innocently, the next day I told my mother about it
> and she got this horrible shocked look on her face and
> as soon as I saw that look on her face I realized that
> something was wrong. . . . She later told me that . . .
> Daddy had made a mistake, that he'd thought that was her
> and not me.

If the mother did anything at that point to stop the father
from repeating such behavior, it was not effective, because
the other daughters had similar experiences with him, as
became apparent years later when one of Sally's sisters ran
away from home and another sister asked Sally if "Dad had
done anything to her."

From Sally's junior high through high school years, the
father's behavior became dramatically worse. Apparent
catalysts were the purchase of a larger home before the old
one was sold, continued growth of the family, and the entry
of the oldest children into adolescence. The children did not
feel as accepting of their father's behavior as their mother
appeared to be, but they were at least as powerless as she to
do anything overt to create any change. Exit from the
situation was still impossible for everyone in the family,
and the potential relief of communication either inside or
outside the family continued to be taboo. However, the
practices of "denial," (Yarrow et al., 1955), "avoiding
and ignoring" (Lynch, 1983:155), and various forms of
withdrawal had become inadequate.

> We knew my father was getting sick because of the way he
> was driving more and more dangerously, on the wrong side
> of the road or trying to force people off the

Sandra goes beyond rote application of course concepts by proposing fantasizing as another accommodative practice. She could make her original idea more relevant to this sociology paper by showing how the psychological process of fantasizing serves some purpose in the family's social interaction.

Here is an example of interview notes incorporated directly into the text.

"Similarly," a "sentence linker" that shows addition, functions here as a transition between paragraphs.

> road. . . . Well, we kids were terrified and sometimes
> my mother would jump out of the car. Sometime we'd yell
> that we were scared. . . .

Thus, at a stage where turning to extrinsic remedies
would have been logical (Emerson and Messinger, 1981:173), it
was believed to be impossible, and there was no choice but to
escalate the coping practices.

All the children began to plan for the time when they
would be old enough to escape:

> The older kids planned escapes by going away to college,
> and the idea was to go as far away for as long as you
> could. I had one sister who ran away because she
> couldn't stand it.

This planning, as the subject describes it, is to some extent
fantasizing, since virtually all the children ended up going
to college at the nearest state university campus.
Fantasizing is an accommodative practice not mentioned by
Lynch (1983) or Yarrow et al. (1955).

Expressions of anger toward the father became
increasingly open. Sally, who worked in the bar where the
father drank, put up with lewd comments in front of the
other customers. But she took great pleasure in counting her
money in front of him at home, thereby reminding him that she
had money of her own while he was deeply in debt. She paid
for many of her own expenses, including clothes, and openly
scoffed at her father when he said he'd pay her back one day.
She "went, literally, for days without speaking to the
man," and the family sat through entire meals without
speaking to one another.

One daughter became anorexic. Psychologically an
expression of self-directed anger, the anorexia also had
another, interpersonal purpose. Sally's interpretation of her
sister's behavior is that "she was going to teach Daddy how
to be disciplined." The sister was "taking over" (Lynch,
1983:158) her father's role as moral teacher, giving him her
child's role as pupil.

Similarly, Sally found herself reversing roles with her
father, "covering for" him (Lynch, 1983:60), and even

The discussion of Sally's "conflict" may be interesting but it is too psychological to be appropriate for this sociology paper.

"taking over" (Lynch, 1983:158) his responsibility as
provider in order to ensure the family's physical survival.

> My father wasn't filling out income tax forms . . . plus
> they had run out of money and they were going to
> foreclose the mortgage . . . and 'cause I was working
> then, my parents borrowed the money from me and I was
> consciously saving my money so that I could leave home
> and never come back and go away to college. . . . My
> father always made my mother do the dirty work. She was
> the one who had to ask me for the money. . . . I was
> crying the whole time. . . . I never expected to see
> that money again. . . .

Sally comments, "and I made my father feel very bad,"
obviously feeling guilty, in spite of his asking for an extra
fifty dollars which she knew was to buy alcohol. This
incident, additionally, illustrates Sally's conflict between
her acceptance of the priority of preserving the family and
her righteous anger at having to sacrifice her own goals.

The mother used her own accommodation practices so that
the family structure could be propped up, to make it appear
as if there were no trouble. One concern was appearance, not
only to people outside the family but also to those within.
This, in turn, served her main goal, which was to maintain
the power structure of the family, as she interpreted it
through her religious and cultural understanding. Through her
determination to preserve the structure of the family at all
costs, Sally's mother limited the responses the family might
make to her husband's troublesome behavior and thus
exacerbated the "organizational havoc" (Goffman, 1981) he
had initiated.

The children were permitted certain practices which
supported the power system their parents had imposed upon
them. As Lynch explains (1983), "ignoring" their father's
oddness (155), "avoiding him" as long as the "integrity of
the group" was not too severely threatened (155),
"covering" (160) and "taking over" (158) for him worked
in various ways on behalf of the family unit. These practices
and those of their mother support Lynch's conclusions about
accommodation practices, that they are "analogous, on a

This transitional sentence both refers back to the previous paragraph and introduces new material.

Here Sandra goes beyond a mechanical application of sociological concepts and demonstrates her understanding of the significance of the presence or absence of certain conditions in the family.

Conclusion clearly stated.

social level, to individual 'Defense mechanisms'"
(1983:162).

However, the obligation to protect the family as a unit
in the manner insisted upon by their parents left the
children sorely in need of a way of coping with their own
resultant "alienation from place" (Cockerham, 1981:246).
They found "meaningful existence is threatened . . . mental
symptoms [and in this family, the accommodation practices
themselves] distort and destroy the very core (that is, love,
affection, respect, loyalty, responsibility) of what makes
those [family] relationships viable" (Cockerham, 1981:245).
The seven children were making great personal sacrifices to
sustain an entity that was not providing them with the
sustenance promised by its definition.

The children were unable to seek emotional support from
either inside or outside the family. They were denied the
group accommodative practices such as "humoring" the
troublemaker, sharing stories, and laughing about him, which,
as described by Lynch (1983:156,159) and Lemert (1962), might
have served to reduce his power and to "constitute a
supportive moral counterpoint" (Lynch, 1983:159).

After cooperating to protect their family, Sally's
family members were left to innovate practices as best they
could to deal with their own needs as individuals. Some of
the ways the children found to compensate for the
organizational chaos and emotional deprivation they suffered
in their family were: expressions of anger through avoiding
the father or pointedly evading his attempts at
communication; throwing up to him his decline as a provider;
withdrawing affection and respect; moral indignation;
fantasizing about leaving the family; and, finally, escaping.

In this family we see operating a complex system of
accommodative practices by nine individuals. On one level the
practices attempt to construct a desirable image for a member
who behaves in a conspicuously troublesome way; they defend
the outer integrity of the group. On another level they are a
defense by individuals in the group to prevent their own
emotional and perhaps mental destruction by the exigencies of
the social unit. The individuals may accept the priority of
those exigencies, but if the social exigencies are in
conflict with their own needs, accommodative practices must
be developed to cope with the conflict.

REFERENCES

Cockerham, William C.
    1981   Sociology of Mental Disorder. Englewood Cliffs,
            New Jersey: Prentice–Hall.
Emerson, Robert and Sheldon Messinger
    1981   "The micro–politics of trouble." Pp. 169–179 in
            Oscar Grusky and Melvin Pollner (eds.), The
            Sociology of Mental Illness, Basic Studies. New
            York: Holt, Rinehart and Winston.
Goffman, Erving
    1981   "The insanity of place." Pp. 179–201 in Oscar
            Grusky and Melvin Pollner (eds.), The Sociology of
            Mental Illness, Basic Studies. New York: Holt,
            Rinehart and Winston.
Lemert, Edwin
    1962   "Paranoia and the dynamics of exclusion."
            Sociometry 25(1):2–20.
Lynch, Michael
    1983   "Accommodation practices: vernacular treatments of
            madness." Social Problems 31(2):152–164.
Pollner, Melvin
    1985   Class lecture, October 14.
Yarrow, Marian Radke, Charlotte Green Schwartz, Harriet S.
        Murphy, and Lelia Calhoun Deasy
    1955   "The psychological meaning of mental illness in
            the family." Journal of Social Issues 11(4):12–24.

Chapter 9

THE QUANTITATIVE
RESEARCH PAPER

In a quantitative paper numerical data are collected to answer a sociological question. Since quantitative papers depend on specific techniques of data collection and analysis, this chapter (unlike the previous three chapters) may be most useful to students who have taken or are taking an introductory research methods course.

Most quantitative papers are based on deductive reasoning (see Chapter 1)— that is, the investigator, starting with a theory or with previous research, expects a certain answer to her or his research question. The investigator develops one or more hypotheses with the aim of predicting the results. However, some quantitative papers are based on inductive reasoning. The investigator, unsure of the answer but with some idea of what to look for, sets out to explore a particular topic. Here the purpose is description rather than prediction. No matter which approach is taken, however, the data collected can be represented numerically.

The sample quantitative paper written by Alvin Hasegawa at the end of this chapter illustrates both types of logic. Alvin uses the deductive approach in examining the relationship between student dating patterns and the prestige ranking of the student's fraternity or sorority, and he uses the inductive approach in examining the differential ranking of five date characteristics by high- and low-status "Greeks." Basing his expectation on theory and previous research, Alvin anticipated that prestige ranking would be related to dating patterns. However, his theory did not say anything specific about whether high- or low-prestige students would rate date characteristics in any particular way. Therefore he was not sure how each of the two groups would rate the five date characteristics.

This sample paper, like most quantitative papers, is written in journal rather than essay format (see the section in Chapter 1 on "Developing an Argument: Logic and Structure" for the difference between the two formats). If you are writing such a quantitative paper, divide it into the four major sections discussed below, skipping an extra line or two between sections. Capitalize and center the heading that labels each section (except for the introduction, which needs no heading). Issues that should be covered in each section include:

1. Introduction: After a review of the relevant theory and literature, what sociological question do you feel needs to be addressed? What, if any, expectations (hypotheses) do you have about the answer?
2. Methods: What method did you use in trying to answer your question? How did you select your sample? What measures did you use? What procedures did you follow?
3. Results: What patterns of numerical data did you find?
4. Discuss: What do your data mean? How do they relate to theory and/or previous research? Do the data support or refute your hypothesis?

Although the length of these four sections is generally about equal for published papers with sophisticated methods and analyses, the introduction and discussion sections for student papers are generally slightly longer than the other two sections. However, the relative length of the sections will depend on the amount of detail required by your instructor in describing your methods and results. In addition to these four major sections, other important components of your paper include the title, Abstract, References, and Appendix. These will be discussed later.

Since journal styles vary, ask your instructor which professional or scholarly journal you should use as a guide. Before starting your paper, examine recent articles from the recommended journal. (If none is recommended, use the *American Sociological Review*.) Photocopy, or carefully read through, one or two sample journal articles to use as a model of format and tone. Your paper should not only look professional but sound professional as well. Scientific communication uses a formal prose style.

Collecting and analyzing quantitative data can be time-consuming. Unanticipated problems or events may interfere with these tasks. Start early in the quarter and apportion enough time on your time grid (see Chapter 2) for these, as well as other, tasks.

We have arranged this chapter according to the steps you should follow in writing your paper. For example, although the title and the

Abstract go at the beginning of your paper, you should write them during the final stages so that they describe your entire study. Therefore, we will cover these components at the end of this chapter.

The first step with a quantitative paper is to write the introduction, before collecting your data or selecting your method. The introduction guides your research and helps determine your focus, which is what Alvin Hasegawa discovered. When we asked him about his paper he told us: "When I write I like to start with the Introduction, to work from the beginning to end. That is different than many people who start with the body [methods section] of the paper. . . . I try to make the Introduction creative and interesting. Once I get the Introduction down, the body of the paper flows well."

The purpose of the introduction is to provide a context for the formulation and operationalization of your hypotheses. Writing the introduction involves searching and reviewing the literature, stating the problem, framing a sociological question, and, where appropriate, developing hypotheses.

Writing the Introduction

Reviewing the Literature

Once you decide on a topic, use the sources listed in Chapter 7, such as *Sociological Abstracts* or the *Social Science Citation Index*, to search for similar empirical studies of the topic. Also gather books and articles on the theory you plan to use as a framework for your study. Read and take notes as you would for a library research paper.

In writing your review of the literature, provide enough background material to place the hypothesis in its proper setting. Begin your review with a summary of the theory (or theories) from which your question is derived, specifying its major tenets and focusing on one or two aspects (or major concepts) that you would like to test. Next, discuss each relevant study, summarizing in a few sentences the theoretical approach, major hypotheses, operational definitions (measures), and conclusions drawn in each one. It is often helpful to arrange the studies in chronological order. How do these studies fit together? Do they form a pattern or are they inconsistent? Did they fail to account for an important variable? What direction did they suggest for future research?

Stating the Problem and Choosing a Question

The statement of the problem reveals the gaps or contradictory findings that you found after reviewing the chosen theory and relevant literature. Its purpose is to point out theoretical inconsistencies in need of resolution, methodological problems apparent in the empirical literature, and/or the logical next step research in this area should take. For example, you may want to concentrate on a different interpretation of a theory not adequately tested; set up a critical test of two rival theories; extend the theory to a new population or substantive area; use a new operational definition of a concept; correct the faulty methodology of a previous study; use a different design or method; or include more variables in order to look for possible interactions.

A well-thought-out study which examines the relationship between two variables is better than one which examines many variables superficially. For some class assignments a simple replication of a published study may be sufficient. Be sure to check with your instructor. However, unless your study is a replication, an exact repeat of an earlier study, you must explain how your study differs from previous works, how your study will extend their findings, and what your study will contribute.

Following from the review of the literature, the statement of the problem should suggest questions that need to be answered (for example, "Is education always related to occupational attainment?"). These questions can be refined and developed into hypotheses (for example, "If ethnicity is held constant, an increase in education will be associated with an increase in occupational attainment.").

Stating Your Hypotheses

The hypothesis in a quantitative paper is the counterpart of the thesis in a library research paper. It is a formal statement expressing the relationship you expect to find between your variables. Your literature review and statement of the problem show the logic which led to the development of your hypothesis. They serve as a sort of preliminary evidence. If your reasoning is sound, the numerical data you collect will provide further support for your hypothesis.

The hypothesis should be stated in such a way that it can be unambiguously confirmed or rejected by the results. It should also be stated in such a way as to make clear the type (causal or correlational) and direction (positive or negative) of the expected relationships. That is, does your hypothesis postulate that one variable causes the other, or does it simply state that the two variables are correlated? If the relationship is believed to be correlational rather than causal, are the variables expected to be related positively (as X increases, Y increases) or negatively (as X increases, Y decreases)? Explain how the independent and dependent variables will be operationally defined, that is, the manner in which the variables will be measured. For example, occupational attainment may be operationally defined as whether the job involves the supervision of other workers. (In correlational studies, no distinction is made between the independent and dependent variable.) Be sure to specify your unit of analysis, for example, individuals, groups, institutions, or countries.

As we stated above, if your study is purely exploratory you will not have specific hypotheses. You may simply have a question which suggested itself as an interesting problem in need of further investigation. In this case you should explain why you feel that exploring this topic is important. For some topics, a descriptive study is often an important first step leading to the formulation of a good deductive study.

Developing a Methods and Analysis Plan

Once you have drafted the introduction (except for the operational definitions of your variables) you are ready to proceed with the development of a methods and analysis plan. (Later, after you have completed the rest of your paper, you will revise and polish your introduction.) Conducting a sound investigation is crucial to writing a good quantitative paper. Therefore, it is necessary to consider in advance all the decisions you must make in collecting your data. Drawing up a methods and analysis plan will greatly improve the quality of your paper and will certainly make the writing process go more smoothly. Although it is beyond the scope of this book to discuss the multitude of methodological and statistical factors that need to be considered in conducting a good quantitative study, we do address those issues important to writing a good report of your study. These tips should be useful to both the novice and the more experienced student. However, if you are currently taking a research methods or statistics course, or have taken one or both in the past, you might want to consult your text(s) for further details.

You will be limited to certain methods depending on the kind of question you are trying to answer. For example, if you are interested in the mortality (death) rates of upper- versus lower-class men, you obviously would have to use archival sources rather than a survey. Your choice of method will also be influenced by your assignment and time and cost constraints. Below, we briefly describe the most common methods: archival sources, structured observation, experiment, and survey.

Archival sources are records of preexisting data. Although some of these data are obtained from surveys—the census, for example—we include them as archival because the results are published in tables available in government documents and books. Most of these data consist of official records of "rates," such as birth, death, marriage, divorce, crime, suicide, and accident rates. For example, you may want to examine the change in divorce rates from 1950 to 1984, the crime rates in urban versus rural areas, or the suicide rates of males versus females. To obtain these data consult a reference librarian (also see Chapter 7).

Structured field observation is different from ethnographic field research because the former is guided by set hypotheses or specific measurement objectives. Structured observation can often involve simple counting, for example, counting the occurrence of certain behaviors or the number of people in different situations. For instance, you may want to observe the frequency with which men as compared to women make supportive statements during group discussions; or count the number of students who use the coffeehouse for studying at different times during the day.

There are many different experimental designs, but the basic model involves two groups—an experimental and a control group. Both groups are treated exactly the same except for the independent variable(s) which is manipulated. Although we usually think of experiments as conducted in a laboratory, experiments can also be conducted in everyday settings (called field experiments). For example, you may want to examine whether people in a shopping mall will be more likely to come to the aid of a well-dressed or a shabbily dressed victim. You could manipulate the situation so that in half the cases your confederate (accomplice) comes to the mall wearing a suit, and in the other half wearing dirty jeans and a torn T-shirt.

The survey method includes both questionnaires and interviews. The logic of the survey is to replicate the experimental method artificially, although without the same degree of control, by comparing two or more groups. The groups can be based on response scores (for example, those who score high or low on a particular attitude measure) or demographic characteristics (for example, Catholics and Protestants, blacks and whites, young and old, high and low socioeconomic status). If you are interested in the different responses of males and females to a series of questions, your independent variable would be sex of respondent. In a survey, unlike an experiment, the independent variable is not manipulated. Instead, the researcher focuses on response differences that result from the naturally existing differences in the respondents.

Whichever method you choose, be sure that your proposed research is in line with the guidelines set forth by the Human Subjects and Ethics Committee on your campus (ask your instructor for details). You may need to get approval for your project from this committee.

Once you have decided on a method, draw up a plan for data collection and analysis to show your instructor. A methods and analysis plan ensures, *before you collect the data*, that your study will actually provide a test of your hypotheses. Further, it guarantees that you will be able to make sense of your data and analyze them successfully. Many students waste time and effort collecting large amounts of data only to discover later that the data do not provide a test of their hypotheses. Or, they find out that they don't know how to go about analyzing the data. A methods and analysis plan can prevent these problems.

When you write your methods and analysis plan, address those issues relevant to your type of study:

1. What population will you sample? How will you select your sample? If you are conducting a structured field study, what setting did you choose? Do you anticipate any problems in gaining access to the respondents or the field setting? How many respondents (of each type) do you need to question? How many observations do you need to make?

2. What measures will you use? That is, how will you operationalize your variables? How long will the questionnaire or survey take to answer? If you plan on conducting an interview or survey, will you use closed-ended (also known as "fixed-response") or open-ended questions? Closed-ended questions compare to open-ended questions as multiple-choice exams compare to short-answer essay exams. What will be the possible range of the response scale (for example, a five-point Likert response scale) for the closed-ended questions?

If you plan to do a structured field observation, what exactly will you look for? How long should each observation last? What things will you want to have on your observation checklist (the list of things which you intend to count or measure)? For example, if you want to observe differences in how near people of different cultures stand to one another, you might want to have a checklist which includes several different ethnicities and distances.

If you will be conducting an archival study you will need to go to the library to find out the types of data that are available to you. Further, you will need to determine the form in which this data is presented. For example, if you are interested in comparing the birthrates of different religious groups you will need to find out if the birthrates presented in the census tables are broken down by religious affiliation. Librarians can very often help you find what you need.

If you are doing an interview or survey you will need to develop an instrument. Even when conducting an experiment in the laboratory or in the field, you generally will want to interview respondents or have them complete a questionnaire at the conclusion of the experiment. Although it is beyond the scope of this book to discuss all the details of creating a sound instrument, there are some general guidelines which you should consider in order to facilitate the writing of your report. Instructors often expect you to include a copy of your instrument in the Appendix of your paper. It is best to include your instrument in your methods and analysis plan and have it approved by your instructor before you collect your data.

In developing your measures, it is best to begin by looking at those developed by other researchers. Scales exist which have already been shown to be valid and reliable. Many of these scales are reproduced in the appendices of books or journal articles, or appear in *Measures of Social Psychological Attitudes* by John Robinson and Philip Shaver of the Survey Research Center at the University of Michigan's Institute for Survey Research. If you use one of these existing scales, be sure to refer to the name of the scale and its originator in the body of your paper, e.g., "Rotter's Locus of Control Scale was administered to respondents," and include the source of the scale in your reference section.

However, you might want to construct some original questions to use in conjunction with an existing scale, or modify existing questions to better suit the purpose of your study. In constructing your own questions, try to avoid the following pitfalls:

1. Avoid using ambiguous terms or slang. Define your terms. For example, in Alvin's questionnaire (see Table 9-1), he defines what he means by the term "date." Since dating patterns have changed over the years, there may be some confusion as to what he meant by this term had he not clarified this point.
2. Avoid "double-barreled" questions. Questions which contain "and" or "or" (such as "Do you feel that physical attractiveness or attitude similarity are important characteristics in a dating partner?") make it impossible to know whether the respondent views one or both characteristics as important. The way Alvin presented his questions eliminates this problem.
3. Avoid biased questions which lead the respondent to answer in a socially desirable way. For example, rather than asking, "Have you ever had a date?" Alvin asks the question"Have you dated in the last year?" Respondents may be reluctant to say that they have never dated. However, they may feel comfortable saying they have not dated recently.

With regard to other aspects of your instrument, consider the following:

1. If it is not necessary to know your respondent's name, do not ask for it. Anonymous questionnaires are more likely to yield honest answers.

2. Provide adequate instructions about how to answer the questions. For example, Alvin's instructions ("Circle the answer which most closely represents how important each date characteristic is *to you.*") lets respondents know they are being asked for their own opinion, not the opinion they believe to be held by their peer group.
3. Number each question in the questionnaire. Space questions out on the page so that they are easy to read.
4. Be careful about the order in which questions are listed. Put easy questions first and difficult or sensitive questions last.
5. Show respect for your respondents. Thank them for their cooperation and retain the confidentiality of their responses.

Again, Alvin's questionnaire incorporates each of these suggestions.

Alternatively, your assignment may allow you to use not only existing measures developed by other researchers, but their data as well. This is called secondary survey analysis. Many large universities subscribe to the quantitative data library service provided by the Interuniversity Consortium for Political and Social Research (ICPSR). One of the most commonly used data sets provided by ICPSR is the General Social Survey collected by NORC (National Opinion Research Center). Check with your instructor about this data library. If ICPSR services your university, and if its use is acceptable for the purposes of your assignment, your task for the methods and analysis plan would involve the selection of an appropriate data base, and within that the selection of specific questions to be used in your analysis.

3. How long will it take to collect the data?
4. How will you get the data into an analyzable form? For example, have you assigned an appropriate numerical equivalent (for example, no = 1, yes = 2) to the response scales of closed-ended questions? Have you developed a coding scheme for open-ended questions? For example, your coding scheme could involve counting the number of respondents who made some reference to social mobility in response to an open-ended question, or counting the number of times different types of respondents mentioned themes of alienation. Remember that in a quantitative paper you must be able to represent all responses numerically.

If you are an advanced student planning on forming an attitude index or scale from a set of closed-ended questions, will the response scores of any of your questions need to be reversed? That is, before adding the response scores of several questions together to form a single scale, will the response scores of negatively worded questions be reversed so as to bring them in the same direction as positively worded questions? Will you leave the index as a continuous variable or will you divide it at the median so as to compare high and low scorers?

5. How will you analyze the data? Depending on your hypotheses and the level of statistical knowledge required for your assignment, there are different ways to do this. If you haven't taken statistics, the two simplest ways to analyze your data would be to calculate percentages or averages on each variable, independently of other variables. Independent percentages or averages are often quite adequate for reporting the results of an exploratory study.

However, in testing hypotheses it is often necessary to look at the relationship between two variables. The complexity of calculating percentages or averages increases when you examine the relationship between two variables because the variables must be examined jointly. Some common methods of doing this include constructing what is called a crosstabulation table (see Tables 1 and 2 in the sample quantitative paper), a table of means (see Table 3 in the sample quantitative paper), or a correlation matrix (not shown). In each type of table one variable is designated as the row variable and the other as the column variable.

Although constructing a correlation matrix would not be feasible, except perhaps for the most advanced student, the beginning student may be able to calculate the crosstabulation table or table of means (averages). For example, in Table 1 of the sample paper, Alvin used the prestige ranking of students' fraternities or sororities as the column variable and the prestige ranking of the dates' fraternity or sorority as the row variable.

In preparing the table, Alvin first rated the prestige level of the respondents' fraternities or sororities. Then, on the basis of this information, he sorted the questionnaires into three piles (high, medium, and low prestige). *Separately for each pile,* he counted the number of respondents who reported dating a student from a high-medium-or low-prestige Greek organization. He repeated this procedure for each pile, producing a set of frequencies to be used in calculating the percentages. At the top of each column in Table 1 Alvin specified the number of students from high- ($N = 10$), medium- ($N = 10$), and low- ($N = 10$) prestige Greek organizations. This let the reader know that the denominator used in calculating the percentages for each pile was "10." For example, he found that out of the 10 high-prestige students, 8 reported dating another high-prestige student ($8 \div 10 = 80\%$), 1 a medium-prestige student ($1 \div 10 = 10\%$). At the bottom of each column, Alvin included the total percentage so that the reader would know how to read the table (for example, $80\% + 10\% + 10\% = 100\%$).

In Table 3 of the sample paper, Alvin calculated averages instead of percentages. He used student status as the row variable and the five date characteristics as the column variable. Again he designated in parentheses the number of respondents in each status category. This

Table 9-1 Example of a Survey: Questionnaire for Alvin's Paper

Questionnaire # _____

Student Dating Questionnaire

The following questionnaire is anonymous. Your answers will be held in strictest confidence.

Please circle your answer to the following questions.

1. What is your sex?
   a. male
   b. female
2. Do you belong to a university-sponsored fraternity or sorority?
   a. yes
   b. no

Using the five-point scale (1 = not at all important, to 5 = extremely important), please circle the answer which most closely represents how important each of the following date characteristics are *to you*.

	Not at All Important				Extremely Important
3. Physical Attractiveness	1	2	3	4	5
4. Personality	1	2	3	4	5
5. Sense of Humor	1	2	3	4	5
6. Potential Occupational Success	1	2	3	4	5
7. Attitude Similarity	1	2	3	4	5

Please circle your answer to the following question:

8. Have you dated in the last year (that is, gone out for purely social purposes with the possibility of developing a romantic involvement)?
   a. yes
   b. no

Thank you for taking the time to complete this questionnaire. Your cooperation is greatly appreciated!

---

time Alvin sorted the questionnaires into four piles (Greek male, Independent male, Greek female, Independent female) according to the respondent's status. Then, *separately for each pile*, Alvin added together the numerical scores given by every respondent for each date characteristic. He divided each sum by the number of students in the pile. For example, the responses of the 15 Greek males in pile 1 for the date characteristic "physical attractiveness" summed to 66 (5 + 3 + 2 + 5 + 4 + 5 + 4 + 3 + 5 + 5 + 4 + 5 + 5 + 4 + 4 + 3 = 66). Alvin divided 66 by the number of the respondents in the pile to obtain the average score (66 ÷ 15 = 4.4). Alvin repeated this procedure for each date characteristic.

Try to make a mock table for analyzing and presenting your results. That is, try to specify which variable you will use as your row variable and which variable as your column variable. Which variables will you use to sort respondents into piles? Determine whether the numbers in the cells will be percentages or averages.

If you are required to carry out more sophisticated statistical analyses of your data, determine the level of measurement of your variables (nominal, ordinal, interval, or ratio). This will allow you to decide which statistical tests can be appropriately calculated. Computer software packages that calculate social science statistics are available for microcomputers. Check with your instructor.

Don't proceed with your data collection and analysis until your instructor has approved your methods and analysis plan and answered questions. Once you complete your data collection and analysis you are ready to begin writing the other sections of your paper.

Writing the Other Sections of Your Paper

The Methods Section

The Methods section directly follows the introduction. It should contain three subparts: Sample, Measures, and Procedure. Each part should be labeled with an underlined heading at the left margin; capitalize only the first letter (see sample paper). Begin by describing your sample.

Describing your sample   Specify the population studied. Discuss in detail how you selected your sample from this population. Did you randomly select respondents, that is, give every member of the population an equal chance of being included in the sample, or did you select whomever you could get? If respondents were randomly selected, describe the steps you took to ensure randomness—for example, tossing a coin or systematically selecting every fifth residence. If you are a more advanced student, did you stratify your sample on any particular variable?

Describe all the relevant characteristics of your sample (for example, age, sex, race). If you had to eliminate any subjects because of incomplete data, or for other reasons, state the number and the reason. Specify the final overall sample size and the size of each group.

Describing your measures   If you obtained your data from secondary sources, describe where the original data came from and how they were measured. If you did a structured observation, describe the behaviors, types of people, situations, etc. that you observed.

If you used a questionnaire or interview, state whether the questions were closed-ended or open-ended, newly developed by you, or adapted from previous research. If you used existing scales or indexes, include information about their validity and reliability, if available. "Validity" refers to the extent to which the questions actually measure what they are supposed to measure. "Reliability" refers to the stability of measurements taken at different times.

In the body of the paper, quote the actual question(s) used to operationally define each variable. If several questions were used, as in the construction of an index or scale, give a sample of the questions and include the others in a table or an Appendix. For example, "Sex role attitudes were measured by agreement-disagreement with 20 statements, such as 'The woman's place is in the home' and 'I would vote for a woman presidential candidate' (see Appendix)." If the questions were closed-ended, state the range of the response scale and describe the anchor points. For example, you might state that you used a five-point Likert response scale ranging from "(1) not at all" to "(5) extremely." If you averaged several questions together to form an index, state what a high and low score on the index signifies. For example, "A high score on the sex role index indicates liberal sex role attitudes; a low score indicates conservative attitudes." If the questions were open-ended, describe the coding scheme that you used to code the data.

Describing your procedure Identify the method you used. Describe when (time of day, day of week, date), where (the geographic location, type of institution, building), and under what circumstances the study took place. This information is especially important if the study was conducted in a field setting.

If you conducted an experiment, be sure to also specify the design. Discuss the procedure by which the independent variable(s) was manipulated and the instructions given to respondents in each group. Specify any additional precautions taken to control extraneous variables and/or exclude bias from your sample. For example, did you randomly assign respondents to experimental conditions? (Random assignment to groups is different from random selection.) If you employed confederates (accomplices), describe who they were and what they did, and whether or not they were kept "blind" (ignorant) to the hypotheses.

Whichever method you chose, summarize each step you took in collecting your data. A good rule of thumb is to describe your methods in enough detail that another researcher could replicate your study.

The Results Section

Discuss how you examined the relationship between your variables. Did you count the number of people who gave each type of response, or did you average the scores of several people? If you calculated per-

Table 9-2 Sample Table

Table 1
Sex Role Attitudes by Sex of Respondent

		Sex of Respondent	
		Male (N = 100)	*Female* (N = 100)
Sex Role	Liberal	55%	85%
	Traditional	45%	15%
		100%	100%

centages or took averages, state the number of people used as the denominator in your calculations.

If you have a large amount of data to report, consider displaying it in a table or figure. Put each table or figure on a separate page at the end of the paper, just before the References. For tables, center the table number at the top of the page with the descriptive title underneath it, so that the reader can tell what is in the table without having to refer to the text (see Table 9–2 for an example). For figures, the descriptive title goes below the graph or diagram and is left-justified (starts in the farthest left column—see Figure 9–1). In the body of the paper, refer to the table or figure by number; then explain it. Remember that the numbers never speak for themselves.

Another way to present your results is to use graphs or charts. You can draw these by hand or you can use one of the many computer graphics programs that are available for both mainframe and personal computers. Although there are too many to mention them all, the best known are SPSS-X or SPSS-PC (formerly known as the Statistical Package for the Social Sciences), or SAS (Statistical Analysis

Figure 9-1 Sample Figure

Figure 1. Measurement Model of Sex Role Attitudes

System), which can also be used to perform statistical analyses. Often visual aids can more dramatically show the relationships between variables. Whether you use a bar chart, a line graph, or a causal model will depend on the type of data that you have and the analyses you perform. Ask your instructor for suggestions on the best way to present your results.

If your assignment required statistical analyses, state the statistical tests performed, their critical values, degrees of freedom, significance levels, and the direction of the results. For example, "The relationship between sex role attitudes and sex of respondent is reported in Table 1. The results of a chi-square test indicate that a significantly greater proportion of females (85%) than males (55%) hold liberal sex role attitudes ($\chi^2 = 24.24$, d.f. = 100, p < .01)." In the Discussion section, you will take this explanation a step further.

The Discussion Section

In the Discussion section you should tie your results back in to your hypotheses. Did the data support your hypotheses? Remember that the statistical significance of your findings does not indicate the theoretical, substantive, or practical significance of your findings. The latter is a judgment you must make in the Discussion section. What does a relationship between X and Y mean in the larger theoretical context? How do your findings compare with previous research? What has the study contributed to the existing body of literature on this topic? What are the practical implications of your findings, if any? What ethical issues were raised?

What is the internal and external validity of your study? That is, to what extent did your study provide an adequate test of your hypotheses? To what other populations can your findings be generalized? Discuss any methodological or design flaws, particularly if your hypotheses are not supported. Make suggestions for improving future research. If the study was methodologically sound, how can you account for your unexpected findings? Do the data support an alternative theory?

What conclusions can you draw? What direction should further research on this topic take?

The Title

Now that you've competed the main sections of your paper you will be able to come up with a good descriptive title. It should be short (rarely over 12 words), and include the theoretical perspective taken and/or the major variables examined (both independent and dependent, where appropriate). See the guidelines for Typing and Submitting Your Paper in Chapter 11.

Abstract

The Abstract, about 100–200 words, is a very brief summary of your paper. It describes the problem, method, sample, results, and conclusions of your study and should contain only ideas or information already discussed in the body of the paper. The Abstract goes on a separate (labeled) page right after the title page. For a heading, type **ABSTRACT** (all in capital letters) and center it. Triple space between the heading and the body of the Abstract. Indent the first line. Although almost always included in a journal article, an abstract may not be required by your instructor.

References

If no specific journal style is required, follow the guidelines in Chapter 4. Your References should include only those sources you actually cited in the body of your paper.

Appendix

The Appendix is optional. Some instructors may want you to include your raw data, your statistical calculations, a copy of your questionnaire, your observation checklist, your instructions to respondents, or other items. The Appendix goes after the References.

Suggested Reading

Babbie, Earl R.
    1973   *Survey Research Methods.* Belmont, CA: Wadsworth Publishing Co. Inc.
Bailey, Kenneth D.
    1987   *Methods of Social Research.* New York: The Free Press.
Fowler, Floyd J.
    1988   *Survey Research Methods.* Newbury Park, CA: Sage Publications.

A Sample Student Paper

The following sample quantitative paper, a study of college student dating patterns, was written by Alvin Hasegawa for an undergraduate class in quantitative research methods in the spring of 1985. Choosing a date may seem like a very personal issue, but this study and others like it reveal that this individual decision is shaped by sociological factors such as class background and membership in particular organizations—for example, sororities and fraternities.

Alvin's assignment required him to work in a group with other students in designing a study, constructing measures, collecting data, and tabulating results. However, each student was responsible for writing her or his own report of the research, so this is an individual paper based on a group project. Alvin and his co-workers discussed their methods and analysis plan with the instructor before they collected their data to ensure that they were on the right track.

Alvin reviewed relevant literature on dating and developed his main thesis to answer questions raised there. The group retested other researchers' hypotheses that dating among Greek students (members of sororities and fraternities) and Independent students is homogamous, a sociological term which means that partners are chosen from within the same social group. They went beyond other studies by also asking students to rank the importance of various characteristics of a dating partner. Thus, this work is located within ongoing discussion but also contains something original—both important considerations in designing sociological research.

The paper, following a journal article format (see "Developing an Argument: Logic and Structure" in Chapter 1), is based on quantitative results from a survey. Notice that it is organized into the major sections described above: title page, Abstract, Introduction that includes a review of the literature, Methods, Results, and Discussion. Alvin has also provided tables that present important results in an easily read format. Our comments on facing pages detail additional important features of the paper as well as ways in which it could be improved.

OUR COMMENTS

Because of the length of his paper, Alvin included a title page as suggested in Chapter 11.

The title "Dating" is not very descriptive. The title should reflect the major variables being investigated. A more appropriate one would be "Homogamous Dating among Greeks and Independents."

Dating

Alvin Hasegawa
Sociology 109
Professor Roseann Giarrusso
May 27, 1985

In the Abstract, Alvin provides a brief summary of his paper. He describes the problem, methods, results, and conclusions of his study. He includes only ideas and information discussed in the body of the paper.

ABSTRACT

According to Waller (1937), dating among university students is based on the "rating-dating complex." However, other researchers suggest that the dating patterns of students are more complex and may actually follow the principle of homogamy. A survey study of university students was conducted to examine these two theories. A total of 68 students responded to questions about the prestige ranking of campus Greek organizations, their own dating patterns, and the importance of five date characteristics. The responses of male and female Greek (members of fraternities and sororities) and Independent (non-Greek) students were compared. The results revealed that the Greek system is stratified on the basis of prestige and that members of the Greek system do date in a homogamous manner. In addition, it was found that the dating patterns of Independents also reflect their social background. Finally, the results revealed that Greeks and Independents differentially rank the importance of five date characteristics. It was concluded that student dating patterns follow the principle of homogamy.

Alvin locates his study in the larger body of literature on marriage and the family. Also, by discussing Waller's classic study he shows that his research question is rooted in a long-standing sociological tradition.

As suggested in Chapter 10, Alvin uses the phrase "in contrast" as a transition between paragraphs.

Here, Alvin shows how the positions of Reiss and Krain et al. differ from Waller's. These studies try to show the limitations of Waller's earlier work. Alvin briefly refers to the theory, hypotheses, methods, and results of these two studies.

Most of us hope that someday we will find that perfect someone whom we will marry. But, in order to accomplish this task, we must go through that courtship system commonly known as the marriage market. Thus, in order to select a mate, we must first go through the dating process. Our group study focused on this aspect of marriage and the family.

In our search for existing data, we came across two important studies. The first was done by Reiss (1965); the second, by Krain, Cannon, and Bagford (1977). Both studies were based upon earlier work done by Waller (1937) on the "rating-dating complex" on college campuses. According to Waller, casual dating among Greeks (members of fraternities and sororities) is a prestige contest based mainly on factors such as having a car, money, and nice clothes, and belonging to the best fraternity/sorority. However, this status-seeking pattern isn't true for seriously dating couples whose goal is mate selection.

Reiss (1965), in contrast to Waller, hypothesized that the Greek class system and related dating actually reflect parental class background. This pattern of dating supports the principle of homogamy because it encourages marriage among those who are similar in social background. To test this hypothesis, Reiss used two surveys: one to rank the Greek organizations and a second to obtain information on Greek dating patterns. He found that most of those in high-ranking Greek organizations had fathers in high occupations (executives, etc.). This was less true in the low-ranking Greek organizations. In the second part of his study, he found that high-ranking Greeks tended to date other high-ranking Greeks, whereas low-ranking Greeks dated elsewhere. This finding supported his hypothesis and showed how parents unintentionally achieve homogamy.

Krain et al. (1977) hypothesized that "stratified prestige structures [do] exist to differentiate Greek organizations from each other" (666). They also believed that dating would tend to be confined within the levels of such structures. Unlike Waller, however, they assumed that serious as well as casual dating would reflect prestige homogamy. With this, they developed two surveys: one on perceptions of Greek organizations' prestige and a second on dating patterns

A review of three studies is not "thorough." Alvin should either acknowledge that the review was very selective or state that there were few studies conducted on this topic (which, in this case, is not true).

Here, Alvin states three hypotheses, clearly and in a way that can be unambiguously confirmed or rejected.

Here he introduces some new questions.

Replication means more than just using the same method. Alvin should have specified exactly how his study is the same.

How many of each group? How many of each sex? What age range? Were students given self-administered questionnaires or face-to-face interviews?

Alvin included the questionnaires in an Appendix (not included in this book, however, for the sake of brevity).

among those with Greek affiliation. They found support for both of their hypotheses in the analysis of their results.

After a thorough review of the literature, we decided to retest the hypotheses formulated by these earlier researchers. Our first two hypotheses dealt with the Greek system here at UCLA. Based on Krain et al.'s (1977) study, our first hypothesis was that Greek systems will be stratified in terms of hierarchical prestige ratings. Our second hypothesis was that those in the Greek system will tend to date in a homogamous manner based on the prestige ranking of their Greek organizations. Our third hypothesis tied in with Reiss's (1965) work, but instead of dealing with Greeks, it concerned "Independents"—non-Greek UCLA students. Thus, our third hypothesis was that parental class background will be reflected in the dating patterns of Independents. Finally, we decided to ask some questions not included in either of the above studies on the rank-order importance of five characteristics in a dating partner. Since we did not have any hypotheses about these characteristics, these questions were just exploratory.

METHOD

Design

Because we chose to use hypotheses previously tested, we simply replicated the research design, i.e., we used the survey method.

Respondents

We surveyed a total of 68 students from two separate groups: Greeks and Independents.

Measures

We constructed two different survey instruments (see Appendix). The first would be used to place the Greek organizations into ranks, according to prestige. The second survey would be used to measure, for both Greeks and Independents, demographic information, dating patterns, and the rank-order importance of five characteristics in a dating partner.

The word "data" is plural, not singular. Therefore, the verb should be plural: "The data were . . ."

Anyone? How were the subjects selected? This section is very weak. Alvin should have given enough detail for another researcher to replicate his study.

Here Alvin tries to control for bias in the data analysis.

Where are the data? He should have included them in a table.

Alvin refers the reader to the table, then explains what the numbers in the table mean.

Procedure

After completing the surveys the next step was to collect the data. The data was collected over the weekend of April 21, 1985. The first survey, which asked students to rank-order the various Greek houses on campus, was given to anyone who had knowledge about the fraternities and sororities. This survey was given to 15 Greek individuals. Our second survey, measuring dating patterns and the importance of the five characteristics, was administered to both Greeks and Independents. This survey was given to 30 Greeks (15 males and 15 females) and 23 Independents (15 males and 8 females). The Greek participants were surveyed at their respective houses, while the Independents were surveyed at the dormitories.

RESULTS

In analyzing our first survey, student rankings of his/her own organization were excluded from the results in order to control for partiality toward one's own Greek organization. We found that the Greek system was indeed stratified, as our data showed a clear-cut view of the separate classes. Each house fell neatly into one of three categories: high, medium, or low. There seemed to be a consensus as to which houses were at the top and which were not.

Our second survey on homogamous dating patterns had to be analyzed separately for Greeks and Independents, owing to the different criteria on which prestige was based for each group.

In our analysis of Greeks, we used the results of the first survey to divide students (based on their Greek membership) into high, medium, or low prestige. Of the 30 Greeks surveyed, an equal number of males and females (5 each) came from high-, medium-, and low-ranking fraternities and sororities. The results are reported in Table 1. We found that Greeks in the high-prestige organizations tended to date other high-prestige Greeks. Those Greeks in the medium-prestige range dated both within their own category

Unless your instructor says otherwise, each table should go on a separate page at the end of your paper, just before the References, rather than in the body of the paper.

Very good table. In order to test his hypothesis, Alvin crosstabulates two nominal level variables to examine their relationship.

Where are the data on sex differences? Again, he should have included these in a table.

Alvin details exactly how social class was calculated and refers to the source of this formula.

The cutoff point used to divide subjects into categories is specified.

It was a good decision to analyze the data separately for males and females, since the females were all upper class.

Table 1
Prestige Ranking of Member's Greek Organization by Prestige
Ranking of Date's Greek Organization

		Prestige of Member's Greek Organization		
		H (N = 10)	M (N = 10)	L (N = 10)
	High	80%	40%	10%
Prestige of	Medium	10	50	20
Date's Greek				
Organization	Low	10	10	70
	Total	100	100	100

and with those in higher categories. For those in the
low-prestige organizations, our results showed that they
dated within their own category. These findings were
characteristic of both males and females in the Greek system.
We also noted that women in high-prestige categories did not
date any less-prestigious Greeks, and the low-prestige men
did not date any higher-ranked Greeks.

Next, we had to analyze the data from our Independent
subjects. In order to get prestige rankings for students in
this group, we used a measure that reflected parental class
background. There were two questions on the survey which
inquired about their father's occupation and education. Using
this information and a social class rating formula, we could
determine social class ratings. The formula was:

(Occupational Rating × 7) + (Educational Rating × 4)
= Social Class Rating.

(See King and Ziegler, 1975, for a description of this
formula.) We decided that any score of 60 and above would
rank in the upper-class/high-prestige category. Anything
below 60 would fall into the lower-class/low-prestige
category.

Of the eight female Independents, none fell into the
lower-or middle-class category. However, in classifying the
male Independents, we were able to separate them into upper
and lower classes. Therefore, we decided to analyze the
results separately for male and female Independents.

Again, nice presentation of the results. The column and row variables of the table are clearly labeled and a descriptive title is provided. For each row, the size of each group is specified in parentheses and the total percent is included so the reader will know how the table should be read.

This type of statement relating the size of the group to the conclusion should go in the Discussion section, not the Results.

Subjects may have found the response categories 1 to 5 confusing since they were asked to rank (rather than rate) each characteristic.

Table 2

Prestige Ranking of Independent Females and Males by Prestige
of Date

Prestige Ranking of Independents	Greeks	Prestige of Date		Total
		Independent/ Off-Campus	Don't Date	
Upper-Class Females (N = 8)	25%	50%	25%	100%
Upper-Class Males (N = 9)	56	33	11	100
Lower-Class Males (N = 6)	0	50	56	100

Table 2 shows that 50 percent of the female Independents
date Independent or off-campus males, i.e., nonstudents,
although our hypothesis would have predicted a similar number
dating Greeks (since the females are of high social class).
However, because of the very small sample size, these results
are inconclusive.

We also see from Table 2 that a large number of male
Independents date both Greek and Independent females in the
upper-class category. In the lower class, note that none of
the Independent males date Greek females, and half of them do
not date at all.

Finally, we analyzed the results of the rank-ordering of
the five characteristics in a dating partner. We did the
analysis separately for males and females, Greeks and
Independents. Subjects ranked each characteristic on a
five-point scale from "(1) not at all important" to "(5)
extremely important." In Table 3 we show the average ranking
of each characteristic, for each subgroup. We can see that
the scores for all five characteristics for females, whether
Greek or not, are the same. Both Greek and Independent
females ranked personality as most important, and potential
occupational success as second most important. For the
males, the results are quite different depending on their
Greek affiliation. Greek males rated physical attractiveness
as the most important characteristic, whereas the Independent

Alvin constructs a table of means to determine whether any differences exist between males and females or Greeks and Independents in terms of the importance of various characteristics of a date.

Again, the verb should be "were," not "was."

In the Discussion section, Alvin reintroduces his hypotheses and states whether they were supported.

Table 3

Average Rankings of Five Characteristics by Male and Female
Greeks and Independents

	Physical Attract- iveness	Person- ality	Sense of Humor	Potential Occupational Success	Attitude Similarity
Greek Males (N = 15)	4.4	3.8	2.9	1.4	2.4
Independent Males (N = 17)	2.6	3.8	2.9	1.3	2.4
Greek Females (N = 15)	2.8	4.2	2.5	3.1	2.3
Independent Females (N = 8)	2.4	3.3	1.9	2.5	2.0

males thought personality was the most important. Physical
attractiveness came in third, after a sense of humor, for
male Independents.

DISCUSSION

Now that all the data was analyzed, we reviewed our
hypotheses. Our first hypothesis, that the Greek system would
be stratified according to prestige, was supported by our
first survey. It showed a consensus of opinion about which
houses belong to high-, medium-, or low-prestige categories.
Our second hypothesis stated that Greeks would tend to date
in a homogamous manner. This, too, was supported. We saw, in
general, that high-prestige Greeks date other high-prestige
Greeks. The Greeks in low-prestige categories also date each
other.

The fact that the medium-prestige Greeks dated both high
and medium Greeks may at first be deceptive. But it too
supports our second hypothesis. Those who dated from medium

Here Alvin offers an interpretation of the results. He introduces the concept of self-esteem and shows how this concept can explain his findings.

This effective transitional sentence reminds the reader what the paper has already addressed and summarizes what's coming next (although all transitional sentences do not have to follow this pattern).

Alvin went beyond replication by bringing in a new set of questions. However, he should have gone further in interpreting the findings.

Here Alvin makes a concluding statement. He relates his findings to previous research and notes the contribution of his study. Note one small, but common, error: although "data" is a plural noun, Alvin uses the singular "has" as its verb. The phrase should read, ". . . and the data have been consistent with previous findings."

Although this paragraph highlights the importance of managing your time, it is irrelevant to Alvin's discussion of his study's weaknesses. Alvin's critique should be directed toward the limitations of his methodology.

to high may have had high self-esteem and perceived
themselves as dating a Greek of similar status.

Our third hypothesis was that the dating patterns of
Independents would reflect their social class background.
Since we assumed that Greek organizations have prestige,
we expected to find that upper-class Independents would date
as many Greeks as Independents, and that lower-class
Independents would stay away from Greeks. Our results seem to
have confirmed this hypothesis. We found that upper-class
Independents were able to date Greeks just as frequently as
they did Independents. And we found that the lower-class
Independents did not date Greeks at all; they stayed with the
Independents or did not date.

In addition to the three hypotheses we tested for, we
had subjects rank five characteristics of a date in order of
their importance. Although we had no clear hypotheses as to
what we could expect, the results were interesting. It is
interesting to note, for example, that "potential
occupational success" was ranked second in importance by all
females. This may imply a female's need for security and a
belief in the traditional role of male support. The results
for the males' ranking of the importance of physical
attractiveness was similar to the females, the Greek males
rated it as the most important characteristic. Are Greek guys
really only interested in a girl's body?

All in all, our results seem to have supported our
hypotheses, and the data has been consistent with previous
findings. Although our research model paralleled others, our
study did add to the previous studies by applying earlier
concepts to a new sample, and by comparing how Greek and
Independent males and females rank-order the importance of
characteristics in a date. However, this is not to imply that
there were no problems with our research. Nothing could be
less true.

Time is a limited resource, and for our group, it was
very precious. Although we had ideas in our heads as much as
three weeks in advance, it wasn't until a week before our
presentation that we got them down on paper. That, perhaps,
was our major downfall, but not our only one.

The survey itself was not perfect. It contained oddly

Alvin should have put quotation marks around the world "casual" and "serious" to indicate to the reader that these were the actual words used in the questionnaire.

This is a common mistake made by students. In scientific communication, "random" means something more than what we mean in everyday language. Alvin also seems to have misunderstood that it is the selection process, not the sample size, that determines the representativeness of the sample.

It is important to be aware of any ethical problems with your study before you undertake data collection. Alvin shows that he was sensitive to this issue.

At the polishing stage, Alvin should have revised to avoid four "he or she" phrases in close proximity. See checklist in Chapter 10 for further explanation.

Unless your assignment requires some discussion of the group processes experienced while undertaking your research project, this type of information should not be included. Also, the informality of the last sentence is inappropriate for scientific communication.

Alvin should have ended his paper by suggesting a direction for future research.

worded questions and vague ideas. A few questions could have
been reworded in order to prevent confusion. In particular,
we might have operationally defined some terms such as casual
or serious dates. Finally, our last question should have read
"rate" instead of "rank." This minor detail could have made a
major difference in our results.

Another problem related to the survey was our sample
population. With only 56 subjects in all, our results could
not have been highly representative. And, although our
subjects were chosen at random, it was not completely random.
Since we sampled residents of only one floor of the dorm, the
results may only reflect the attitudes of students on that
floor and not the entire UCLA population.

As far as ethics are concerned, this research was pretty
fair. Our surveys were anonymous, so no one would feel as if
they were giving up intimate secrets for everyone to see. The
only ethical issue that might arise would be if a subject
discovered that he or she was in a low—prestige ranking or if
he or she found out that he or she did not date. Of course,
the subject knows whether he or she dates, but the survey may
rub it in. The realization that one does not date may result
in lowering self—esteem.

In conclusion, our group made up for our problems with
our effort. Although we could have (and should have) started
earlier, we didn't. But that didn't stop us. We all worked
hard,and with cooperation, we finished our project fairly
successfully. Now that we're through, we can all relax, and
go out and find some dates.

REFERENCES

King, Michael, and Michael Ziegler
    1975   Research Projects in Social Psychology: An
            Introduction to Methods. Monterey, Calif.:
            Brooks/Cole Publishing Co.
Krain, Mark, Drew Cannon, and Jeffery Bagford
    1977   "Rating-dating or simply prestige homogamy."
            Journal of Marriage and the Family 39:663–674.
Reiss, Ira L.
    1965   "Social class and campus dating." Social Problems
            13(2): 193–205.
Waller, Willard
    1937   "The rating-dating complex." American Sociological
            Review 2:727–735.

Alvin includes in his Reference section only the sources he actually cited. Also, he
follows the format recommended in Chapter 4.

PART III

FINISHING UP

It has long been an axiom of mine that the little things are infinitely the most important.

SHERLOCK HOLMES IN CONAN DOYLE'S
"The Adventure of the Copper Beeches"

Chapters 10 and 11 of this book will help you complete the paper-writing process. Although we encourage you to read this section before you begin your paper, it will be especially helpful after you have typed your second draft and before you type the final copy.

Chapter 10 tells you how to fine-tune. After you type your second draft, get away from it—for several days if possible, for a good night's sleep at least. Efficiency in spotting weaknesses increases dramatically with distance from the paper, and flaws that escape your bleary eyes at 2:00 A.M. often leap off the page when you are rested.

At the fine-tuning stage, the most difficult parts of the writing process are behind you. In fact, some writers who do anything "to avoid writing the first word" (see the quotation at the beginning of Chapter 2) actually *enjoy* polishing. Think of polishing as a way of showing hospitality, and your reader as a special guest whom you would not dream of putting to work. For example, bring a fuzzy argument into sharp focus; at points where you have moved abruptly from one point to another, supply transitions, connecting the components of your argument for your reader; and correct punctuation, citation errors, and spelling so as not to confuse or distract.

How important is punctuation? And why does the very word often provoke negative feelings? Rudolf Flesch comments in *The Art of Plain Talk:* "Punctuation, to most people, is a set of arbitrary and rather

165

silly rules you find in printers' style books and in the back pages of school grammars. Few people realize that it is the most important single device for making things easier to read" (Flesch, 1962:108). But negative feelings also arise from lack of confidence in manipulating punctuation (and other matters of style, such as sentence structure). Style manuals (mentioned in Chapter 3) can help, but if you enjoy learning from people more than learning from reference books, investigate writing courses at your college. Some colleges attach adjunct writing courses to sociology and other courses.

Chapter 11 supplies guidelines for a step in the writing process that really matters, the presentation of your paper. In some cases, your paper will be among dozens that your probably overworked instructor must evaluate. Imagine your own irritation if, after reading students' papers for hours, you picked up one that was typed with a faint typewriter ribbon that should have been replaced long ago; or, conversely, imagine your sigh of relief and gratitude when the next paper in the stack is easy to read. Although a nicely presented paper that lacks substance will not likely fool even the weariest instructor, studies reveal that a professional-looking paper implies a smart and serious student and often contributes to a better grade. Taking the time to "package" a carefully written paper also shows respect for your instructor's workload—a respect he or she may well be inclined to return.

At this stage you are on the last lap, but do not underestimate the importance of a strong finish. Therefore, allow ample time for careful—not rushed—polishing, typing, and proofreading. Following the suggestions in our last two chapters can turn "poor" into "satisfactory," "good" into "excellent."

CHECKLIST FOR POLISHING YOUR PAPER

1. Can you quickly identify your thesis—that is, your central argument?

2. Does your thesis remain evident and central throughout the paper?

3. Do you support your thesis with adequate evidence? One trick for checking the quantity and quality of your evidence is to put a mark in the margin of a rough draft wherever you see evidence for your thesis, pausing at each point to review its validity. Instructors sometimes use this method when evaluating the soundness of an argument.

4. Is there a clear, logical relationship among all the paragraphs? If one is irrelevant to your thesis—no matter how dazzling—delete it; if one wanders from the topic, bring it back into line. Stick to the subject.

5. Repeat 4 (above), substituting "sentences" for "paragraphs."

6. Does the writing flow back and forth between generalizations and specifics that support and clarify those generalizations?

7. Are there transitions between paragraphs? Sometimes transitions seem to create themselves naturally during the writing process. Other times you have to create them, very deliberately, at the polishing stage. But make them look natural, not slapped on. The smoothest transitions, perhaps, come in the first sentence of each paragraph, deftly referring back from where you came and forward to where you are going. Your reader will be grateful for transitions because the ride through the paper will be smooth, not bumpy.

8. Now pay attention to transitions between sentences. Sometimes the logical connection between sentences is clear without adding anything. However, there are some common words and phrases for ma-

neuvering between sentences, sometimes called "sentence linkers," that you already use, probably unconsciously, in your writing and daily conversation. Consider inserting a few of the following sentence linkers, using appropriate ones. If you use ones you do not fully understand, you might diminish rather than enhance the quality of your paper.

- *To show addition:* again, also, and, and then, besides, equally important, further, furthermore, moreover, next, similarly, too, what's more.
- *To show time:* after, afterward, as, at length, at once, at the same time, by, earlier, eventually, finally, first, formerly, gradually, immediately, later, next, once, previously, second, soon, then, thereafter, while.
- *To make the reader stop and compare:* after all, although, at the same time, but, conversely, for all that, however, in contrast, in the meantime, meanwhile, nevertheless, nonetheless, notwithstanding, on the contrary, on the other hand, still, whereas, yet.
- *To give examples:* as an illustration, for example, for instance, in other words, to illustrate, to demonstrate.
- *To emphasize:* as a matter of fact, clearly, in any case, in any event, in fact, indeed, more important(ly), obviously, of course, that is.
- *To repeat:* as I have said (demonstrated, argued, noted, etc.), in brief, in other words, in short.
- *To draw a conclusion:* accordingly, as a result, at last, consequently, hence, in brief, in conclusion, in sum, on the whole, so, therefore, thus, to conclude.

9. Do all your words mean what you think they mean? For those occasional moments of doubt, we recommend your owning a good hardcover dictionary (the College Edition of *The American Heritage Dictionary of the English Language* is one good choice) as well as a portable paperback if you sometimes write and study in the library. As we mentioned in Chapter 3, be especially careful when using terms that have become part of everyday language and yet retain special sociological definitions (the examples we gave were "stereotype," "status," and "self-fulfilling prophecy"). If you're uncertain about the sociological definitions of your key terms, you might find them quickly in sociology textbooks by using the index and/or glossary. Several dictionaries of sociological terms are also available.

When dealing with words that do not have special sociological meanings, a thesaurus can help you both to locate the most precise word that expresses what you want to say and to find synonyms for varying your word choice. The popular paperback *Roget's College Thesaurus,* in dictionary form, is simple to use because words are alphabetized just as they are in a dictionary. However, before you use a synonym from a thesaurus in your paper, check its meaning in a dictionary. Mark Twain said that "the difference between the almost right word and the right word is really a large matter—'tis the difference between the lightning-bug and the lightning." Believe it or not, the search for "just the right word" can be fun.

10. Have you looked carefully for errors in style (sentence structure, punctuation, spelling, citation)? As we mentioned in Chapter 3, reference books which present style guidelines are available in most bookstores and libraries. Now, at the polishing stage, it may be valuable to consult such a source. *The Chicago Manual of Style* and Kate L. Turabian's *A Manual for Writers of Term Papers, Dissertations, and Theses* are reputable manuals, but your instructor may recommend another. See Chapter 4 for one citation format used widely in sociology.

11. What about contractions (for example—it's, don't, you're)? If occasionally or consistently using contractions feels more natural to you than writing the words out (it is, do not, you are), then ask if your instructor objects. If you have waited until the last minute and do not know your instructor's preference—which may vary according to the assignment—then play it safe and avoid contractions (for example, they are not appropriate for the journal format).

12. Have you stated your conclusion clearly and forcefully?

13. Have you inadvertently used sexist language (for example, used the masculine pronoun "he" exclusively)? Many writers would prefer to use nonsexist language, but repeating "he or she" (or "she or he") every time a singular pronoun is required can sound awkward and repetitive. An occasional "he or she" sounds fine; but two in one sentence or, say, three in one paragraph are distracting. Sometimes writers "solve" this problem but create another by following a singular noun or pronoun with the non-gender-specific, but plural, pronouns "they" and "their." For example, here is a paragraph from Alvin Hasegawa's paper in Chapter 9.

As far as ethics are concerned, this research was pretty fair. Our surveys were anonymous, so no one would feel as if they were giving up intimate secrets for everyone to see. The only ethical issue that might arise would be if a subject discovered that he or she was in a low-prestige ranking or if he or she found out that he or she did not date. Of course, the subject knows whether he or she dates, but the survey may rub it in. The realization that one does not date may result in lowering self-esteem.

In what looks like an admirable attempt to write in a nonsexist manner, Alvin erroneously changes a singular pronoun to a plural one ("so no one would feel as though they . . .") and then uses four *he or she's* in close proximity. In many cases you can easily manipulate language so that it is both nonsexist and grammatically correct by using plural subjects, which can be followed, quite correctly, with "they" or "their." Here is one possible revision of Alvin's paragraph:

> Ethically, this research was pretty fair. Our surveys were anonymous, so respondents would not feel as if they were giving up intimate secrets for everyone to see. The only ethical issue that might arise would be some subjects' discovering that they were in a low-prestige ranking, or if they found out that they did not date. Of course, the subjects know whether they date or not, but the survey may rub it in, resulting in lowered self-esteem for some respondents.

Chapter 11

TYPING, FORMATTING, AND SUBMITTING YOUR PAPER

First impressions count. What your paper *looks* like is important. Its appearance will create expectations in your instructor who picks it up to read and grade. A professional-looking paper promises quality. So take the necessary trouble at this last stage. Find out your instructor's preferences, if any, about format, including title page, citation, and appendix(es), if applicable. Unless your instructor specifies otherwise, follow these fairly standard guidelines:

Typing

If You Are Using a Typewriter

Use a reasonably new typewriter ribbon. Clean your typewriter keys, if necessary. You do not want the instructor remembering your paper as the one with annoyingly faint print or the one with all the *e's* and *o's* filled in.

Type on sturdy white paper (not onionskin or erasable). Instructors do not like erasable paper because they find it difficult to write comments on it. If you really must use erasable paper because you are a poor typist, then photocopy your paper and give your instructor a good photocopy. Leave margins of one to one-and-one-half inches on all sides.

Double-space throughout the text of the paper, except for quotations longer than five lines, which should be single-spaced and indented five spaces from the left margin. (Do not indent the right-hand margin.)

After typing the final copy of your paper, proofread, proofread again, and have someone proofread it for you. Look for errors in punctuation and spelling, typos, and omissions. Some sentence-structure problems can be easily fixed, even on the final copy. For example, a sentence fragment might be made into a complete sentence by inserting a word or two, although generally it is not acceptable to insert more than a few words by hand.

Despite your best efforts, you may need to make some corrections on the copy you turn in. Correction fluid and correction tape are some of the products available for making "clean" corrections at the typewriter. However, some corrections may have to be made in ink.

Here are some of the most common corrections, which can be made in ink by using conventional proofreaders' marks. You may want to combine some of these commonly understood proofreaders' marks with your favorite correction method; for example, you may prefer to use correction fluid to white out a misspelled word rather than strike it out as is suggested below. Most instructors are more concerned with the end—corrections that are instantly intelligible—than the means.

To insert, put a caret (∧) just below the line at the place where you want to insert and then write in the word or phrase directly above the caret.

Example: This is what you do if you have left $\overset{out}{\underset{\wedge}{}}$a word or phrase.

To delete, put a single line through the word or phrase.

Example: the ~~good~~ word

If you omitted a space while typing, draw a vertical line between the words you want to separate.

Example: the|word

If your typewriter has skipped a space in the typing of a word, close the space with a pair of horizontal parentheses.

Example: typ‿ing

If letters need transposing, do this:

Example: the typing

If you have badly misspelled a word, draw a single line through it and write the correction directly above it. If you have omitted only one letter, insert it by using a caret.

Example: accom_∧odate

If you have failed to indent a paragraph, put the paragraph sign (¶) right before it.

If You Are Using a Computer

Begin by setting up the following automatic features for your paper. Use the tabs, not the space bar, for measurement (for example, one inch, not eight spaces) so that the format remains constant when you print out your text, even if you change fonts, pitch, or typeface.

- margins (one to one-and-a half inches on all sides)
- double-spacing (quotations longer than five lines will be single-spaced and indented one inch from the left margin)
- paragraph indentions (one-half to one inch)
- left justification. Do not justify the right side; a ragged right is friendlier and the spacing between the letters often looks better.
- a header with your last name and page number only

Open two files so you can access, and move information between, two corresponding windows: (1) your notes and/or outline and (2) your developing draft of the paper.

Embed a symbol system as you keyboard your paper which you can use later to locate passages easily with the search command. This means use something like XXX to identify a place or places that you will want to find later, for example, to illustrate a point, explain an illustration, or to go back to later to complete a thought. Always refer to labels and figures by writing out the number ("Table One"). In that way you can use the universal "Search For" and "Replace" functions later to renumber them if necessary.

Scrutinize your paper for unintentionally repeated passages. A common problem in word-processed papers occurs when a writer copies and moves a chunk of text but forgets to delete the original.

Use your spellchecker. There is no excuse for misspellings or other mistakes in word processed papers. There should be no handwritten corrections on a word-processed paper. Make corrections at the keyboard and then print out another copy, depending on the number of corrections and their complexity, or you might prefer to print out a hard copy, correct it, and then enter the corrections.

Find out if your program includes a thesaurus and/or a style analyzer, and use them.

Word processing turns writers into designers. The creative possibilities of printing out a final draft, once the completed draft has been saved in the computer's memory, can be very satisfying. Here—especially on the Macintosh—is an opportunity to experiment with typeface, pitch, font, italics, boldface, boxes, borders, underlining, etc. Unfortunately, the result is sometimes a mess and distracts the reader from your ideas. To avoid this problem, keep these design principles in mind:

- Make the shape follow sense. What you do to the printed words should emphasize their meaning. For example, Helvetica Narrow 12 point is excellent for tables and other types of writing that require lots of information in a very small space. Zapf Chancery is a display face which gives headings a decorative look. New Century Schoolbook looks traditionally academic.
- Use restraint. If you emphasize everything, nothing stands out.
- Use your page preview function or scroll through the document to identify and repair "widows," which are single lines separated from the rest of their paragraph by a page break, or other breaks such as captions separated from figures.
- Stick with 12-point fonts. Smaller ones are hard to read, especially on a dot matrix printer. Since legibility is important, use a reasonably new ribbon or cartridge.
- Use your italics function to indicate titles of publications which on typewriters need to be underlined.
- Simplicity is best. Just because you can create elaborate headers and footers, for instance, doesn't mean that the reader needs all that information.

Many programs allow you to import figures from other files into your paper, but if you feel overwhelmed by the technology, you can manually cut and paste them into the appropriate place in your paper, and photocopy the page.

As with any work on a computer, save your document often and back it up on another diskette or a hard disk. For insurance against hardware problems, make an extra copy on a floppy disk.

Formatting

If you use a title page, center your title horizontally and place it halfway down the page. In the lower right-hand corner type your name, the course number (for example, Sociology 101), the name of your instructor, and the date. Number pages beginning with the first page of the text, not with the title page. Sometimes instructors do not require a title page for short papers (approximately five or fewer pages). If you're not using a title page, provide the same information (your name, the course number, the instructor's name, and the date) in the upper right-hand corner of page 1; triple-space and center the title; and triple-space again before you begin the first paragraph.

A quick review of Chapter 4 will remind you of the proper form for citing sources in the text of your paper and for References or Bibliography, a list which follows the text.

Depending on the type of paper you've written, some instructors may want you to include your raw data, statistical calculations, a copy of your questionnaire, observation checklist, instructions to respondents, ethnographic field notes, or other items. As appropriate, you should make each of these items an appendix to your paper (*The American Heritage Dictionary* defines "appendix" as "supplementary material.") The appendix belongs after the References or Bibliography on a separate, titled page. If your paper requires more than one appendix, number or letter each one (Appendix 1, Appendix 2, etc. or Appendix A, Appendix B, etc.) Number pages of the appendix(es) as if they were additional pages of the text—if, for example, the last page of the text is numbered 5, the first page of the appendix would be 6.

How you should space an appendix (single, double, etc.) depends on the nature of the material and how it can most easily be read; spacing need not be the same for all appendixes. However, the heading will ordinarily be centered and triple-spaced—that is, you triple-space between "Appendix" and the title and triple-space again between the title and the body of the appendix.

Submitting Your Paper

Fasten the paper with one staple, not a paper clip. Do not use a cover or folder, which creates unnecessary bulk for your instructor's briefcase and unnecessary expense for you.

Keep a photocopy of your paper to insure against loss or misunderstanding.

Thinking Big

If you and/or your instructor is particularly pleased with the quality of the paper you produced, you might consider submitting it for presentation at a national or regional meeting of a professional sociological association or for publication in a scholarly journal. Paper presentations and publications, which demonstrate good communication skills, will increase your chance of getting into graduate school and will also enhance your résumé.

The main professional organization in sociology is the American Sociological Association (ASA). ASA holds an annual national meeting for the presentation of both theoretical and empirical research. Usually several sessions are devoted to undergraduate and graduate student papers. The international sociology honor society Alpha Kappa Delta (AKD), also holds both regional and national meetings in which students have the opportunity to present their work. Ask your instructor or undergraduate counselor for more information about these and other professional associations.

You might also consider submitting your paper for publication in a scholarly journal (see Chapter 6 for a partial list of these journals). Always look inside the jacket of the latest issue of the journal for the name and address of the current editor and the guidelines for submission. Ask your instructor how to draft a cover letter to accompany your paper submission.

Suggested Reading

Mitchell, Joan P.
   1989   Writing with a Computer. Boston: Houghton Mifflin Co.

REFERENCES

Becker, Howard
   1984   Writing for the Social Sciences. Chicago: University of Chicago
           Press.
Durkheim, Emile
   [1897]   Suicide. Glencoe, IL: Free Press.
   1951
Flesch, Rudolf
   1951   The Art of Plain Talk. London: Collier.
Fowler, Henry W.
   1965   A Dictionary of Modern English Usage. 2nd edition. Ernest Jawer,
           ed. New York: Oxford University Press.
Galbraith, John Kenneth
   1979   "Writing, Typing, and Economics." Atlantic Monthly. March:
           102–105.
Lanham, Richard
   1979   Revising Prose. New York: Scribner's.
Mills, C. Wright
   1959   The Sociological Imagination. New York: Oxford University
           Press.
Olson, Gene
   1972   Sweet Agony. Grants Pass, OR: Windyridge Press.
Stark, Rodney
   1985   Sociology. Belmont, CA: Wadsworth
Turabian, Kate L.
   1973   A Manual for Writers of Term Papers, Theses, and Dissertations.
           4th edition. Chicago: University of Chicago Press.
University of Chicago Press
   1982   The Chicago Manual of Style. Chicago: University of Chicago
           Press.

ABOUT THE AUTHORS

The members of the Sociology Writing Group came together in 1984 to prepare a guide for instructors and students in sociology and writing courses at UCLA. *A Guide to Writing Sociology Papers* grew out of this collaborative effort. Judith Richlin-Klonsky and Ellen Strenski coordinated the group's work and edited the book.

Roseann Giarrusso holds an M.A. and a Ph.D. in sociology from UCLA, and also has an M.A. in psychology. As an instructor and teaching associate, she has taught a variety of courses in both fields, and has conducted workshops on how to succeed in college through skills development. She is currently a Research Associate at the University of Southern California, where she conducts research on intergenerational family relations. Roseann Giarrusso contributed major portions to Chapters 2 and 3; Chapter 9 is her work.

Judith Richlin-Klonsky is a Ph.D. candidate in sociology at UCLA and holds an M.A. in family therapy. Her research interests focus on gender segregation in the history of mental health professions and on the work of mental health professionals. She has worked with undergraduates in a variety of courses, including social control, the sociology of mental illness, medical sociology, and the sociology of the professions. Judith Richlin-Klonsky contributed major portions of Chapters 1, 4, 6, and 7. Chapter 8 is her work.

William G. Roy is an Associate Professor of Sociology at UCLA, where he received the 1989 University Distinguished Teaching Award. He specializes in comparative-historical sociology, specifically long-term political and economic transformations. His current research seeks to explain the rise of American industrial corporations at the turn of the century. William G. Roy wrote the "Framing a Question" and "Developing an Argument: Logic and Structure" sections of Chapter 1 and contributed to the development of the chapter as a whole and to Chapter 6.

Ellen Strenski received her Ph.D. from the University of Reading, England and is Assistant Director of UCLA Writing Programs where she coordinates writing across the curriculum. She has designed and taught writing courses attached to a variety of academic disciplines, including sociology. In addition to co-authoring *The Research Paper Workbook* (New York: Longman, 3d. ed., 1991) and *Making Connections Across the Curriculum: Readings for Analysis* (Boston: Bedford Books, 1986), she has published in many pedagogical journals on the subject of writing in diverse disciplines. Ellen Strenski contributed major portions to Chapters 3, 4, 5, and 7, and contributed to Chapter 6.

ABOUT THE CONTRIBUTORS

Constance Coiner is an Assistant Professor of English at the State University of New York, Binghamton, and a member of the editorial board of *Radical Teacher*. Her book-length study of the Old Left and feminism as they intersect in the lives and literature of Tillie Olsen and Meridel Le Sueur is forthcoming from Oxford University Press. Constance Coiner contributed major portions to Chapters 2 and 3 and contributed to Chapters 4 and 5, and to Part III.

Arlene Dallalfar received her M.A. and Ph.D. in sociology from UCLA. She has been a teaching assistant in diverse courses ranging from social theory to mental health and has been the consultant to teaching assistants for two years in the Department of Sociology at UCLA. Arlene Dallalfar contributed to Chapter 7 and to the list of specialized reference sources for sociology.

Lisa Frohmann is a Ph.D. candidate in sociology at UCLA, Her areas of research include law and society and feminist theory. She has been an instructor in sociology, women's studies, and communication studies. Lisa Frohmann contributed to Chapter 6 and to the index.

Nancy A. Matthews received her Ph.D. from the Department of Sociology at UCLA, where she specialized in political sociology, social movements, and gender, writing a dissertation on the anti-rape movement. She has taught courses in gender, women's studies, deviance, and race relations at several colleges in the Los Angeles area. Nancy A. Matthews contributed to Chapters 1 and 6, the Introduction to Part II, and the introductions to the student papers.

INDEX